100 THINGS
JETS FANS
SHOULD KNOW & DO
BEFORE THEY DIE

Bill Chastain

TRIUMPH
BOOKS

Triumph Books and colophon are registered trademarks of Random House, Inc.

Library of Congress Cataloging-in-Publication Data

Chastain, Bill.
    100 things Jets fans should know & do before they die / Bill Chastain.
        p. cm.
    One hundred things Jets fans should know and do before they die
    ISBN-13: 978-1-60078-522-1
    ISBN-10: 1-60078-522-0
    1. New York Jets (Football team)—Anecdotes. 2. New York Jets (Football team)—MIscellanea. I. Title. II. Title: One hundred things Jets fans should know and do before they die.
    GV956.N37C43 2010
    796.332'64097471—dc22
                                                2010032739

This book is available in quantity at special discounts for your group or organization. For further information, contact:
    Triumph Books
    542 South Dearborn Street
    Suite 750
    Chicago, Illinois 60605
    (312) 939-3330
    Fax (312) 663-3557
    www.triumphbooks.com

Printed in U.S.A.
ISBN: 978-1-60078-522-1
Design by Patricia Frey
All photos courtesy of AP Images.

For Jets fans everywhere

Contents

1 Joe Namath

Joe Namath put the New York Jets on the map, simple as that.

The Pennsylvania native came to the Jets from the University of Alabama, where he played for legendary coach Paul "Bear" Bryant and earned the reputation as a bad boy after Bryant suspended him at the end of his junior season.

Namath suffered a major knee injury in his senior year at Alabama, but that did not keep the St. Louis Cardinals of the National Football League from drafting him with the 12th pick of the draft, nor did it keep the Jets from using the first pick of the American Football League Draft to select the strong-armed quarterback. Both drafts took place on November 28, 1964.

Namath's decision to play for the Jets only added to his renegade image, which included long hair, white shoes, and a playboy lifestyle. The NFL and AFL were just beginning a revolutionary period for pro football in which bidding wars from both leagues were conducted to sign players. Eventually the NFL would figure out that the prudent move would be to merge with the rival league, but that did not happen before Namath signed with the Jets for a record-setting salary of $427,000.

Namath, New York, the AFL, and the antiestablishment movement of the 1960s were perfectly suited for one another, which resulted in Namath becoming more than just a football player. One segment of the public embraced the Jets quarterback for his antics away from the football field, while Jets fans simply adored what he did on the field.

Namath earned AFL Rookie of the Year honors in 1965 after he threw for 18 touchdown passes. Popular among his teammates,

1

Namath First to 4,000 for a Season

Joe Namath opened eyes with his passes during his first two seasons in the AFL in 1965 and 1966, but what he accomplished in his third season had been thought to be unreachable for quarterbacks.

Namath completed 164 of the 340 passes he threw as a rookie for 2,220 yards, and he followed up in his second season in 1966 by completing 232 of 471 passes for 3,379 yards. So the 24-year-old quarterback from Alabama had more than familiarized himself with the AFL by the time the Jets kicked off the 1967 season against the Buffalo Bills on September 10, 1967.

Opening on the road, the Jets lost 20–17 to the Bills, and Namath did not do particularly well, as he completed just 11 of 23 passes for 153 yards. Week 2 brought a different story when Namath completed 22 of 37 for 399 yards in a 38–24 win at Denver against the Broncos. The chemistry that had developed between receiver Don Maynard and Namath was reflected in Maynard's four receptions for 141 yards that day.

The following week the Jets played their home opener at Shea Stadium, and Namath went off against the Miami Dolphins, completing 23 of 39 passes for 415 yards and three touchdowns. After three games, Namath was close to 1,000 yards for the season, having passed for 967.

Opposing teams began to load up their defenses with one purpose in mind: stopping Namath.

And the Oakland Raiders managed to hold him to 166 yards through the air in the fourth week of the season, but the Jets had won the game 27–14. Then Namath struggled against the Houston Oilers when he completed 27 of 49 passes for 295 yards. Just one of those passes went for a touchdown, while he threw six interceptions in a 28–28 tie.

Namath had already surpassed the 3,000-yard barrier when the Jets hosted the Kansas City Chiefs in their 12th game of the season on December 10. He completed just 14 of 25 passes for 133 yards that day, which made the idea of him reaching 4,000 yards look unreasonable.

But Namath rebounded by throwing for 370 yards against Oakland on December 17, leaving him 336 yards shy of the elusive 4,000-yard barrier.

The Jets traveled to San Diego to play the Chargers on December 24, and Namath was at his best. He completed 18 of 26 passes for 343 yards with four touchdowns and no interceptions in a 42–31 win. Namath finished the season with the unheard-of total of 4,007 yards, making him the first quarterback in professional football history to surpass the 4,000-yard barrier.

Namath became "Broadway Joe" after teammate Sherman Plunkett started calling him that. The name perfectly suited his flamboyant image, but the image would not have worked if he had not been getting it done on the field also.

During the 14-game 1967 season, Namath became the first quarterback in professional football history to surpass 4,000 passing yards in a season, with 4,007. He continued to battle his knee problems throughout his career, but that did not stop him from earning AFL All-Star status in 1965, 1967, 1968, and 1969.

Namath's legacy continued to grow until reaching a crescendo in the 1968 season by leading the Jets to an 11–3 regular-season mark followed by a 27–23 win over the Oakland Raiders in the AFL title game. Namath threw three touchdown passes that day to earn the Jets a spot in the Super Bowl against the Baltimore Colts.

Sports fans perceived the NFL to be the superior league when the Jets and Colts headed for the 1969 Super Bowl in Miami. The perception had some merit, because NFL teams had claimed wins in each of the first two Super Bowls. Unconventional and brash, Namath didn't see a difference between the leagues and wasn't intimidated by the Colts, a team that had dominated the NFL during the 1968 season. He said as much during the buildup for the big game, guaranteeing a Jets win. And in what is viewed by many as the biggest upset in football history, Namath led the Jets to a 16–7 win.

Weeb Ewbank, head coach of the American Football League's New York Jets, takes a look at Joe Namath—the team's $400,000 quarterback from the University of Alabama—during a light workout on Namath's surgically repaired knee in New York on June 29, 1965.

Injuries began to take their toll on Namath after the 1969 season, which was reflected in his missing 30 of the team's games from 1970 through 1973. The Jets floundered without their leader and did not have a winning season during that stretch.

Namath would rekindle his magic on occasion during his waning years with the Jets, but the injuries never freed him to achieve his full potential. The Jets waived him in 1977 so he could sign with the Los Angeles Rams.

Namath retired after the 1977 season and was enshrined into the Pro Football Hall of Fame in 1985. While Namath's numbers never reached the heights that his ability suggested he should reach, he was a special player who arrived at the perfect time.

"He was a guy that came along and broke a lot of the conventions," former teammate John Dockery said about Namath on

ESPN Classic's *Sports Century* series. "He was like a rebel with a cause. It was like traveling with a rock star. He just was a magnet. He's attracting people, and mostly young people. And talk about excitement and energy. Wow!"

2 Super Bowl III

Conventional wisdom backed the National Football League heading into Super Bowl III.

The Baltimore Colts from the established NFL would be pitted against the American League Football champion New York Jets, a team believed to be inferior and from an inferior league and that threw the ball around like a circus act.

Baltimore had dominated the NFL, steamrolling to a 13–1 record while outscoring their opponents 402–144. The Colts had advanced to the Super Bowl with a 34–0 thrashing of the Cleveland Browns in the NFL Championship Game, which further established them as a team many believed to be one of the best ever. On top of that, the NFL had won the first two NFL-AFL Championship Games in lopsided contests that experts pointed to as an indication of one league's superiority over the other. So the outcome of the Super Bowl was a foregone conclusion.

Meanwhile, the Jets did not have quite as easy a time navigating the AFL. Yes, they finished 11–3, but many of their games had been close against opponents deemed to be of far lower quality than those in the NFL. Oddsmakers saw Super Bowl III as yet another mismatch and christened the Jets as 18-point underdogs.

Joe Namath wasn't buying it.

Miami's Orange Bowl hosted Super Bowl III, and the city was abuzz with talk about how the Colts would run roughshod through the Jets to once again prove the NFL's superiority. Talk of the thrashing the Jets would take eventually stuck in Namath's craw to the point where he barked back at a man who heckled him about the Jets' chances during a banquet. Namath shot back, "We're gonna win the game; I guarantee it."

Oddly enough, Namath's confident statement did not get a lot of coverage, though sports heavyweights Edwin Pope of the *Miami Herald* and Howard Cosell, who had a radio program in New York City, each noted Namath's bravado in the face of what seemed to be overwhelming odds.

Cosell managed to play both sides of the fence, closing his radio show the day before the game with, "Joe has never disappointed me before, so I'm going with the Jets in tomorrow's game." Cosell then picked the Colts to win big when asked his opinion the following day on a network pregame show.

In addition to Namath's bold statement, the Jets had players who were NFL retreads, such as future Hall of Famer Don Maynard, who had played for the Giants; cornerback Johnny Sample, who had played for the Colts; and Jets head coach Weeb Ewbank, who had been the Colts' head coach.

The game took place on January 12, 1969, and the Colts appeared to be the better team at the outset. The Jets received the opening kickoff and were forced to punt after gaining just 15 yards on five plays. After taking over at their own 27, the Colts drove the ball to the Jets' 19, where the drive stalled and ultimately resulted in no points when Lou Michaels missed a 27-yard field goal.

A palpable momentum shift could be felt after Michaels' miss, and the Jets got busy probing the Colts' highly touted defense that focused on stopping the Jets' deep threat Maynard, who, unknown to the Colts, played with a tender hamstring. The fact that the

Big Play Biggs

At 6'4" and 275 pounds, Verlon Biggs gave the Jets a mountain of a man when they drafted him out of Jackson State in the third round of the 1965 AFL Draft.

Biggs had a soft-spoken manner off the field, but he was a dominating force on the field, giving the Jets the perfect bookend to Gerry Philbin at the other end. He became a three-time All-Star and was voted the outstanding defensive player in the 1966 AFL All-Star Game.

A fierce competitor, Biggs' strong suit was rushing the passer. Long before Mark Gastineau ever charged a quarterback while wearing the green and white, Biggs became a vision of the storming defensive end tormenting the quarterback. And he made two of the biggest plays in team history, both of which came during the 1968 season.

First came a huge play against the hated Oakland Raiders in the 1968 AFL Conference Championship Game, the winner of which would advance to Super Bowl III to play the Baltimore Colts.

Late in the game, the Raiders faced a fourth-and-10 when dangerous Daryle Lamonica dropped back to pass. Biggs burst through the line to sack the Raiders' quarterback, thereby preserving a 27–23 lead.

In Super Bowl III the Jets led 7–0 at the half, which allowed the skeptics to still believe that the Colts would come back to win. But on the first play from scrimmage in the second half, Biggs set the tone for the defense—and the upset—by forcing a fumble, which set up a Jets field goal, thereby adding steam to the Jets' 16–7 upset win.

Biggs' last season with the Jets came in 1970, when he played out his option in advance of signing with the Washington Redskins, where he played through 1974. He spent the 1975 season on the injured list and then retired. After leaving the game, Biggs became a professional wrestler for several years before operating a small farm.

Biggs died on June 7, 1994, which made him the first player from the Jets' 1969 Super Bowl champion team to do so.

Weeb Ewbank, who coached Biggs on the 1969 Jets championship team, spoke at Biggs' funeral, calling him a great team player "who was always where he was supposed to be."

Colts keyed on Maynard allowed George Sauer to experience one-on-one coverage for most of the game. Namath exploited that fact, connecting with Sauer for eight completions, good for 133 yards. Meanwhile, running back Matt Snell continued to run between the tackles, beating up the Colts' line to give the Jets the much-desired balanced attack.

Snell scored on a four-yard touchdown run at 9:03 in the second quarter to give the Jets a 7–0 lead, and they held a 16–0 lead early in the fourth quarter. The Colts bounced back to score a late touchdown, but they could not make a successful comeback, and the Jets had a 16–7 victory.

Namath completed 17 of the 28 passes for 206 yards and came away with the MVP trophy, even though a good argument could have been made for Snell, who rushed for 121 yards on 30 carries. But Namath had been the prophetic one, and when he ran off the field, the Jets quarterback held up the index finger of his right hand to signify that what many had thought to be impossible had just happened: the Jets were No. 1.

3 The Heidi Bowl

One of the best professional football games nobody ever saw—rather, nobody ever saw the ending—came on November 17, 1968, when the Jets played their hated AFL rival, the Oakland Raiders.

Few would have argued that the Jets and Raiders were two of the top teams in the AFL when they met in the Oakland Coliseum that Sunday afternoon. Fans of both teams and those of the AFL in general tuned in for the late-afternoon contest (Eastern Standard Time) on NBC to see who would win a classic matchup between the up-and-coming Jets and the defending AFL champion Raiders. The fact that neither team liked the other served up an extra caveat for viewers on top of the fact they would be watching a marvelous collection of football talent on the field. Ten future Hall of Fame players were in uniform that day, including classic AFL gunslingers Joe Namath of the Jets and Daryl Lamonica of the Raiders, two quarterbacks who were not afraid of putting a little air underneath the football.

Everything about the game lived up to its billing, including the intensity of the game, which produced a violent brand of football that resulted in 19 penalties. Heading into the final minute of play, viewers had been treated to eight lead changes. But due to those penalties and other delays, the game had gone abnormally long. Jim Turner had just kicked a 26-yard field goal to put the Jets up 32–29 with a minute and five seconds remaining in the game, leaving NBC with a dilemma: should they show the remaining 65 seconds, or should they switch to *Heidi*, the much-hyped family movie scheduled to begin at 7·00 PM?

NBC went with the movie, and all hell broke loose—on and off the field.

On the field, the Raiders began their next possession at the 22. Needing 78 yards for a touchdown, Lamonica quickly got to work, hitting Charlie Smith for a 20-yard gain that was augmented by a facemask penalty against the Jets, taking the ball to the Jets' 43.

Jets safety Jim Hudson had been ejected earlier in the game, and the astute Lamonica elected to test his replacement, Mike D'Amato. Smith blew past D'Amato, and Lamonica dropped one of his famed bombs into his hands for his fourth touchdown pass of the day. After the extra point, the Raiders led 36–32.

Had the Raiders scored too quickly? Forty-two seconds remained on the clock, and Namath already had 19 completions for 381 yards. But the Jets quarterback never got the chance to square

Heidi Bowl Casualty

Billy Joe was inducted into the College Football Hall of Fame for his playing career as a running back at Villanova in the early 1960s and for his work as a small-college football coach. He did not enjoy the same success while playing professional football.

Prior to joining the Jets in 1967, Joe played for the Denver Broncos, Buffalo Bills, and Miami Dolphins. His rookie season was his best when the 6'2", 235-pound fullback rushed for 646 yards and four touchdowns and was named the AFL Rookie of the Year.

During the 1968 season, the Jets utilized Joe's talents as a backup for Matt Snell and Emerson Boozer, but that would end in the Jets' 10th game of the season against the Oakland Raiders in Oakland on November 17, 1968. You might have heard of this game; it came to be known as "the Heidi Bowl."

The game became famous because NBC switched from the game telecast to show the movie *Heidi*. During the final 65 seconds of the game, the Raiders scored two touchdowns to earn a come-from-behind 43–32 win. Of more significance to Joe, he took a blow to his left knee that caused torn ligaments, thereby ending his season and, essentially, his career.

"Oakland came back on us, and no one saw me get hurt," Joe told newyorkjets.com. "That was the last of me as a Jet. I ended up staying in the UCLA Medical Clinic for three weeks. Then they flew me back to Lenox Hill Hospital, and I stayed there for three weeks. I had contracted a staph infection."

Ironically, that was the same weekend famed Chicago Bears running back Gale Sayers injured his knee. Sayers managed to make a comeback the following season; Joe did not have as much luck.

Joe played in 22 games for the Jets, rushing for 340 yards on 79 carries and five touchdowns.

things up, as Earl Christy fumbled the kickoff at the 12 and Preston Ridlehuber grabbed the fumble and bolted into the end zone.

A sellout crowd of 53,318 celebrated their team's good fortune—and their own, because they had been able to witness the end of the 42–32 game that concluded at 7:10 PM EST. Viewing audiences on the East Coast had not been so lucky.

The switchboard at NBC lit up with calls from irate fans. Further exacerbating the situation were the reminders of what had happened. An hour and 20 minutes into the movie, NBC ran a streamer across the bottom of the screen that reported the outcome of the game. Later in the movie, the same information crawled across the bottom of the screen, taunting those who were beside themselves for not being able to see the end of the game.

Julian Goodman, the president of NBC, issued a statement that said, "It was a forgivable error committed by humans who were concerned about the children who were expecting to see *Heidi* at 7:00 PM. I missed the end of the game as much as anyone else."

Alas, all was not lost. In the aftermath of the Heidi Bowl debacle, the NFL's contracts with the networks were amended to require games to be shown in their entirety in a team's market area.

Namath-Unitas Passing Shootout

Even though Joe Namath was just 29, he had seen better days by the time the Jets teed it up for the 1972 season. Countless surgeries had taken their toll on the body of the famed Jets quarterback, leaving questions about how much longer he could play.

Meanwhile, Baltimore Colts legendary quarterback Johnny Unitas had grown long in the tooth. The physical tools he'd displayed while beating the New York Giants in the 1958 NFL Championship Game had long passed, but he still had guile and the brains of a brilliant quarterback even at the advanced age of 39.

Always a Deep Threat

From the time Richard Caster joined the Jets in 1970 until he left the team eight years later, the 6'5", 228-pound receiver/tight end was a deep threat.

Caster went to the Jets as their second-round pick in the 1970 NFL Draft (46th overall) out of Jackson State, and he loosened up defenses from the beginning, daring Joe Namath to overthrow him on deep balls.

In his rookie season, Caster played wide receiver, averaging 20.7 yards per catch with three touchdowns, including a long of 72 yards. He also spent his second season with the Jets as a wide receiver and averaged 17.5 yards per catch.

While Caster had been a deep threat as a wide receiver, the Jets felt they had a unique player, given his size and speed, which prompted a change to tight end in 1972. That's when Caster really separated himself while running through the land of linebackers and safeties rather than the speedier cornerbacks.

In his first season as a tight end, Caster had what would turn out to be his best season in professional football when he caught 39 passes for 833 yards and 10 touchdowns, which was good for a 21.4-yards-per-catch average.

Memorable from that 1972 season was the game when the Jets played the Baltimore Colts in Baltimore on September 24. Namath and Johnny Unitas locked up in a passing duel that Namath ultimately won by throwing six touchdowns. Of those half a dozen, three went to Caster, who hauled in touchdowns of 10, 79, and, finally, 80 yards. The last score proved to be the backbreaker in a 44–34 Jets win.

Caster played eight seasons for the Jets, catching 245 passes for 4,434 yards and 36 touchdowns before moving to the Houston Oilers in 1978. He would spend three years with the Oilers, two with the Washington Redskins, and one year with the New Orleans Saints. All told, he played 13 seasons in the NFL.

To Jets fans, Caster will always be big No. 88, the man who always seemed to be behind the defense.

Namath and Unitas clearly were not the quarterbacks they had been in their glory days, but even in diminished form both were still capable of going on a roll. And the pair of quarterbacks—both of whom hailed from Pennsylvania and were headed for the Hall of Fame—brought something special to the field on September 24, 1972, in Baltimore.

After losing to the Jets in Super Bowl III, the Colts had taken each of the next four meetings between the two teams heading into the 1972 contest. A capacity crowd of 55,626 Colts fans showed up to watch the two veteran field generals go head to head.

Namath was making his first-ever start in Baltimore, and he found the turf at Memorial Stadium to his liking.

Broadway Joe burned the Colts' defense for six touchdown passes—one short of the NFL record—while completing 15 of 28 passes for 496 yards. Namath threw the only interception of the afternoon when Don Maynard ran the wrong route, which led Colts safety Jerry Logan to jump the route and make the pick.

Unitas could not match Namath where touchdowns were concerned and threw just two that afternoon. But he managed to complete 26 of the 44 passes he attempted to accrue 376 yards.

In the fourth quarter the Jets were clinging to a 30–27 lead when Namath spotted tight end Rich Caster in the clear and connected with the converted tight end on a 79-yard touchdown strike.

Unitas answered by driving the Colts 83 yards in 10 plays, completing the drive with a 22-yard touchdown pass to Tom Matte, cutting the lead to 37–34.

The Jets got the ball back and began at their own 20 with Namath mulling over his options. Did he need to play conservative, or should he again rear back and let it go? Speaking of that situation after the game, Namath told Dave Anderson of the *New York Times* that he told himself, "If you ain't confident, you don't belong here."

So Namath opted to again throw the ball deep with the Colts blitzing on the play. For the third time that afternoon, he found the open Caster, this time for an 80-yard touchdown to put the game on ice at 44–34.

At the end of the day, Namath and Unitas had combined to set a new NFL record by throwing for 872 yards in an affair still regarded as a passing clinic of the finest order.

5 Bachelors III

Joe Namath ran with a fast crowd and embraced the playboy lifestyle, so sooner or later he was bound to make a move that didn't please the ultraconservative NFL. Ultimately, that move came when he opened Bachelors III.

Namath liked to spend time with the ladies and carouse, which often placed him on barstools in any number of establishments in New York. So he found sound logic in the idea that if he was going to spend time and money at a bar, he should do so at his own place, where he could control his surroundings and profit from his celebrity.

Thus, Namath and two other partners—who were also bachelors—opened the Upper East Side bar named appropriately to reflect the marital status of the partners. And the bar could not have opened at a better time than early in 1969, shortly after Namath's Super Bowl III heroics. He lived as a New York icon and frequently inhabited his bar, which only added to the frenzy of Bachelors III as a hot spot. Crowds had to be turned away, and business couldn't have been better for the budding entrepreneur and his partners.

Bachelors III was a popular nightspot, particularly when Joe Namath was there. Here is the original Bachelors III at 62nd St. and Lexington Ave. in New York on June 24, 1969.

The forecast for continued success prompted plans for future Bachelors III openings in other cities.

Alas, Pete Rozelle did not dig Bachelors III as much as the hip New York crowd. Well aware of Namath's involvement in the bar, the NFL commissioner grew concerned about some of the unsavory characters frequenting the bar owned by the most popular quarterback in professional football. To Rozelle's way of thinking, hanging around in a place with said characters could lead to all kinds of

Mantle Men and Namath Girls

New York sports icons Joe Namath and Mickey Mantle were joined together in business in 1969 with the advent of an employment agency known as Mantle Men and Namath Girls, Inc.

The venture became the personification of athletes failing in business ventures.

Mantle Men and Namath Girls, Inc. was George Lois' brainchild. Lois operated Lois Holland Callaway, a successful two-year-old advertising agency. But Lois and company wanted more, as he explained to the *New York Times* in 1969, saying, "Our concept since we started was to get into other businesses too. We found that there was a tremendous vacuum in the personnel field and decided to get into the job business. We wanted to get the two most popular athletes in New York, maybe the world, as the spearheads of the business. So we asked Namath and Mantle."

Commercials for the fledgling company included TV spots of 10 to 30 seconds that featured Mantle and Namath. In one such spot, Mantle claimed, "Our people are pros." And Namath added, "Just like us."

A launch party for Mantle Men and Namath Girls took place at the swanky Four Seasons restaurant in Manhattan on August 11, 1969. Lois explained at the party that Mantle and Namath, who were also investors in the company, would not operate simply as figureheads.

"They'll be writing letters, cracking hard accounts, having lunch or playing golf with president and chairman of the board," Lois said. "We believe in advertising."

The idea to have Namath and Mantle pitch the product was cutting edge and earned a lot of praise in the advertising business.

Mantle Men and Namath Girls had three Manhattan offices that grossed $2 million in their first year of operation, and Lois looked to expand by signing up franchisers in 12 cities. Eventually the company became the second-largest job-employment agency in the world before a recession hit, which made jobs scarce and, in turn, made it difficult for an employment agency to place its clients.

The company's initial success proved fleeting, and Mantle Men and Namath Girls eventually folded.

problems that might compromise Namath. And just like that, Namath became a target for Rozelle, who cited him for being in violation of several morals clauses in his contract that were familiar to every NFL player. In order for Namath to make everything right, Rozelle decided that Namath needed to sell his interest in Bachelors III or he would be violating his contract. Never could he have anticipated Namath's reaction to his demand.

At a teary-eyed press conference, Namath announced that he would be retiring from football.

In the aftermath of Namath's announcement, the NFL suffered a great deal of anxiety. The Jets quarterback had become the NFL's most bankable player. He brought increased visibility and revenue streams to the league. If any one player could be viewed as the kicker in the deal that brought the NFL/AFL merger to fruition, Namath was the guy. And just like that, he would be gone.

Understanding the magnitude of the situation, Rozelle and the NFL hoped to find a compromise in which both parties could save face. Namath and Rozelle were brought together to discuss the situation, and a lengthy meeting ensued. Namath had agreed to the meeting because he, too, began to imagine what life would be like without football. Not only did he love to play, he loved the trimmings, which included money and a lifestyle befitting a rock star.

And the commissioner and the star quarterback reached an agreement. Grudgingly, Namath allowed that he would sell his interest in the Bachelors III in New York while maintaining his ownership position in other locations.

Two weeks after retiring from football, the NFL's biggest star returned to the gridiron to join the Jets training camp already in progress.

6 Jets Play in First *Monday Night Football* Game

Monday Night Football came into being on September 21, 1970, and the Jets and Cleveland Browns met that evening for what turned out to be a historic launching of a program that would become ingrained into the fabric of the American culture.

Pete Rozelle, the NFL commissioner, had long sought to move NFL games into other time slots of the week for TV. High school football derailed the prospects for televised Friday-night games, but Rozelle remained persistent. He persuaded CBS to air one NFL game during prime time on a Monday night in 1966 and 1967. The AFL had not yet merged with the NFL and had a contract with NBC at the time, so they followed suit with Monday-night games in 1968 and 1969.

Once the two leagues merged, CBS and NBC remained attached to their respective leagues, though they had become the National and American conferences. Given the fact that they had a good product in televising the Sunday games, they did not embrace the necessary gamble to bite on a contract to show weekly Monday-night games. So Rozelle went to ABC to broach the subject with the lowest-rated network about showing Monday-night games. After some dancing, they entered into a contract with the NFL to begin showing NFL games on Monday nights during the fall of 1970.

Everything then fell into place for ABC. Roone Arledge was selected to produce the show, and he felt the broadcast needed more flair, so he hired Chet Forte to be the director, and they shared the vision of bringing a previously unseen entertainment factor to NFL games. Innovations included more cameras, more graphical information, and a three-man crew working the booth rather than the traditional two-man crew. Assuming the role of that trio were Keith Jackson, Howard Cosell, and Don Meredith, who brought more than enough personality and entertainment to the telecast.

In that memorable first *Monday Night Football* contest, the Jets put forth a less-than-memorable performance that saw them set a team record by getting penalized 161 yards. And Joe Namath, though sharp at times as evidenced by his 18-of-29, 284-yard performance, also threw for three interceptions. Matt Snell also performed well, outdueling prolific Browns running back Leroy Kelly by rushing for 108 yards in 17 carries while Jets defenders held Kelly to 62 yards on 20 carries; but Snell also coughed up the football on the Browns' 7.

Despite all the mistakes, the Jets made a game of it with a crowd of 85,703 watching at Cleveland's Municipal Stadium.

Namath hit George Sauer late for a 33-yard touchdown to cut the Browns' lead to 24–21 with just over two minutes left in the game. The Jets' defense then forced the Browns to punt from their 27. Unfortunately for the Jets, Mike Battle then made the biggest mistake of the night for the Jets when he had a chance to field the Browns' punt at the Jets' 30. Instead, he let the ball hit the ground, and it rolled to the 4-yard line, leaving the Jets 96 yards to cover with 90 seconds left on the clock. Namath's third interception of the game followed, and the Browns took a 31–21 win.

Results from the first *Monday Night Football* game were encouraging. The Nielsen scale for the New York City area registered a 21.9 rating, which translated to 1.3 million homes watching, and nationally the game carried a share of over 35 percent of the viewing audience. ABC had paid the NFL $8.5 million for the rights in the first year of a four-year contract and sold out all of its commercial time at $65,000 per minute.

Monday Night Football was well on its way.

7 Steve O'Neal's 98-Yard Punt

In the spring of 1969, the Jets used their 13th-round pick of the NFL Draft to select a punter out of Texas A&M, making Steve O'Neal the 338th selection.

Entering the 2010 season, O'Neal's career punting average of 40.7 yards per kick ranks 11,645th overall among NFL punters since 1950. To say he had a modest career would be a vast understatement. But the former track star from Hearne (Texas) High School set a record during the 1969 season that can never be broken.

O'Neal went to College Station on a track scholarship and probably would not have played college football had a football not found its way onto the track while he ran one day. According to the story, O'Neal picked up the ball and boomed a nice punt back in the direction from which the ball came. Word got around about how he punted, and eventually Gene Stallings, the head coach of the Aggies, found out about O'Neal's prowess. Soon the Aggies had a new punter. In his junior season, O'Neal punted for the Aggies team that won a Southwest Conference title in 1967 before defeating heavily favored Alabama in the Cotton Bowl.

Veteran Curley Johnson had served as the Jets' punter for the previous six seasons when the team selected O'Neal in the draft. Johnson, who punted 68 times during the 1968 season for an average of 43.8 yards per punt, moved across town to the New York Giants, where he spent the final season of his 10-year career.

On September 21, 1969, the Jets were at Mile High Stadium playing the Broncos in Denver's thin air. For O'Neal, the game would be his second as a professional.

The Jets found themselves on their own 1-yard line on a fourth down to force a punt. O'Neal took the snap and then created perfection for a punter.

Kicking out of his own end zone, O'Neal stood just 11 yards from the center rather than the normal 15, stationing himself just inside the back line. Once the ball left O'Neal's foot, he knew he had hit a beauty, which was further validated when he began to roll out from his deep position to help with the coverage. Normally he would see the ball leveling out by that point, but this particular punt brought a different sight, and he noticed the ball was still going up.

The ball traveled 75 yards in the air before hitting the grass, where it traveled another 23 yards before it came to a stop at the 1-yard line.

O'Neal's kick had traveled from the 1 to the 1, establishing a record for the Jets punter that nobody has approached since. Despite O'Neal's heroics, the Jets lost 21–19 to the Broncos.

O'Neal averaged 44.3 yards per punt on 54 punts during his rookie season and did not have a punt blocked.

Players did not make the kind of money they would in later years, and O'Neal always looked toward a future in which he planned to practice dentistry, so he continued to work in the off-season toward earning his dental degree during his first four years of professional football. The closer O'Neal moved toward obtaining his degree, the more nervous the Jets got that they would lose their punter and receive no compensation once he got his degree. Finally the Jets opted to trade him to the Saints prior to the 1973 season. A knee injury made 1973 O'Neal's final season.

Attend the NFL Draft

Jets fans are the Archie Bunkers of the NFL Draft—uh, make that the Meatheads—so attending an NFL Draft live at the Radio City Music Hall is a must for any true Jets fans.

Only when Jets fans do something like throwing snow at Santa Claus do they gain more notoriety than they do on the day of the draft.

Beginning with the 1980 NFL Draft, the selection of players by NFL teams has been a televised event. The draft took place on Saturday and Sunday from 1995 to 2009. Prior to that it was held on Sunday and Monday from 1988 to 1994, and prior to 1988, it took place on one or two weekdays.

Since that first televised draft, the popularity of the event has grown every year to where it is now a three-day prime-time extravaganza. Approximately 39 million people watched the 2010 draft. Along the way, draft gurus such as Mel Kiper Jr. were born, mock drafts became the rage on the Internet, and Jets fans became a major part of the show in the form of comic relief.

Clad in Jets attire, Jets fans have shared a noticeable pattern of behavior that sees them cheer loudly before their pick—often chanting the name of the player they believe the team should select—then booing once the selection is made and it's not the one the Jets fans in attendance have anointed as the chosen one. And, yes, to say alcohol is involved would be a gross understatement.

Jets fans have had to endure many selections that their team has made against their wishes only to see that, had the team listened to its loyal fans, it would have been better off. For example, what if the Jets had selected Dan Marino rather than Ken O'Brien in the 1983 draft? Warren Sapp would surely have worked out better than Kyle

Easy Jets Trivia

Before any Jets fan reads this book, he or she should already know the answers to the following Jets trivia quiz.

1. When the American Football League came into existence, the New York team was not named the Jets. What was the team's original name?
2. Who coached the Jets when they won Super Bowl III?
3. Which Jets running back gained over 100 yards in Super Bowl III?
4. Which Jets receiver wore No. 13 and is in the Hall of Fame?
5. What stadium did the Jets call home during the 1968 season when they made their march toward the Super Bowl?
6. What team did the Jets play in the game that came to be known as the Heidi Bowl?
7. Where did Joe Namath play college football?
8. What was the nickname of the Jets' defensive line that included Joe Klecko, Mark Gastineau, Marty Lyons, and Abdul Salaam?
9. How many Super Bowls had the Jets played in through the 2009 season?
10. What team did the Jets defeat in Super Bowl III?

Answers:

1. Titans	6. Oakland Raiders	9. One
2. Weeb Ewbank	7. University of Alabama	10. Baltimore Colts
3. Matt Snell	8. The New York Sack	
4. Don Maynard	Exchange	
5. Shea Stadium		

Brady in 1994. And in 1989 the booing reached a crescendo when the Jets selected Jeff Lageman, a linebacker from the University of Virginia. Leading up to that draft, Kiper declared Lageman did not have the size to play in the NFL. Jets fans agreed.

So how does a Jets fan go about joining his brethren at the draft? It's not complicated or costly, just time-consuming. Tickets to the NFL Draft are free and are awarded on a first-come-first-served basis after being distributed at the Radio City Music Hall's box office on the morning of the draft. To get the tickets one must endure long lines on the day of the draft, and you can't designate one of your buddies to get the tickets because multiple tickets cannot be handed out to one person; the rules allow one ticket per person.

True Jets fan don't care if they have to wait the day of the draft. Simply put on your Jets jersey, paint your face green, and go with just the right amount of alcohol, and you'll fit right in. Just remember to save your voice in advance of the big event. Booing can be extremely taxing on one's vocal chords.

9 Wesley Walker

Wesley Darcel Walker came to the Jets in the second round of the 1977 NFL Draft.

Possessing soft hands and above-average speed, the former California wide receiver brought along with him a malady most perceived as a handicap: he was legally blind in his left eye.

At age eight, Walker's father first discovered that his son had a vision problem when they were playing catch. Surgery wasn't encouraged, and doctors told him that even if he wore contact lenses and glasses, his vision would still be blurred. He had light perception in the left eye but lacked any depth perception. Walker refused to give in to the problem and relied on his peripheral vision, which allowed him to achieve balance and to sense motion.

Walker still had to overcome a lot. He had trouble judging speeds in Little League and got hit in his left eye, and he had to deal with the cruelties of growing up with the nickname "One Eye." Dealing with the equivalent of having one hand tied behind his back, Walker managed to excel.

Attending Carson High in Los Angeles, he achieved High School All-American honors in 1972 and never played in a losing game. And he used his blazing speed to become the city's 100- and 220-yard champion.

After earning a scholarship to Cal, Walker set an NCAA record by averaging 25.7 yards per catch during a college career in which he caught passes directed at him by future NFL quarterbacks Vince Ferragamo and Steve Bartkowski and the late Joe Roth. Along the way he also hauled in 22 touchdowns while distinguishing himself as a sprinter on the Cal relay team. He earned All-American honors and was recognized as Cal's first four-year dual-sport letterman.

Walker did have 20/15 vision in his right eye that helped overcome his left-eye blindness, but he had problems dealing with the glare from the lights of dome stadiums. And due to the proximity of his left eye, he found that he was better at catching the football when lined up on the left side, where he could run looking for the football over his right shoulder.

Walker was no longer called One Eye once he got to the Jets, but he did gain another nickname: Sammy Davis Jr. By then the sting of any nickname had lost its strength.

In Walker's first year with the Jets in 1977, he set a team rookie record with 740 receiving yards, and he led the NFL in receptions in 1977 and 1978. He hauled in the most catches of his career in 1983 when he chalked up 61 for 865 yards and seven touchdowns. Pro Bowl honors came his way in 1978 and 1982, and he earned team MVP honors in 1978 after leading the NFL in receiving yards.

Walker earned a reputation as a big-play receiver and brought Jets fans many memorable moments.

On September 21, 1986, Walker set a team record for touchdowns scored in a game with four against the Dolphins. His fourth touchdown came at the 2:35 mark of overtime when he hauled in a 43-yard strike from Ken O'Brien to give the Jets a 51–45 win.

Walker caught the longest pass in Jets history on December 8, 1985, when he snared a 96-yard bomb from O'Brien during a 27–7 win over the Bills in Buffalo.

No. 85 retired after the 1989 season with 438 catches for 8,306 yards and 71 touchdowns. He defied the odds to become one of the great players in Jets history as well as one of the most popular players in team history.

10 The New York Sack Exchange

One of the great nicknames in Jets history came into being in the 1980s: the New York Sack Exchange.

The group did not consist of traders looking to take a position on pork-belly futures. Rather they distinguished themselves by trading in muscle, enough muscle to make opposing quarterbacks endure restless nights of sleep before lining up to play the Jets.

The New York Sack Exchange was the nickname for the Jets defensive line that played in the early 1980s: Joe Klecko, Marty Lyons, Mark Gastineau, and Abdul Salaam.

Lyons told the *New York Daily News*, "It wasn't a question of whether we'd get to the quarterback, it was how many times."

Generally, *poorly* would be the consensus if one asked a Jets fan about the way the team has drafted over the years. The group that would come to be known as the New York Sack Exchange brought an exception to that sentiment.

Salaam was a seventh-round selection in 1976, Klecko came to the team in the sixth round of the 1977 draft, and Lyons (first round) and Gastineau (second round) were selected in 1979. Klecko and Gastineau were the defensive ends, while Lyons and

Salaam were the tackles, whose main job was to stop the run. The group's formula for success called for them to shut down the run on first down to force second-and-long and third-and-long situations. Doing so would free the group to pin their ears back and bull-rush the quarterback.

The nickname came via a contest run by a magazine, the *Jets Report*, which called for entrants to name the group. A Brooklyn police officer, Dan O'Connor, became the winning entrant with the name the New York Sack Exchange.

O'Connor recalled the contest in an article on *Bleacher Report*, when he said, "I thought, *What goes good with New York?* New York Stock Exchange; New York Sack Exchange. It was perfect."

In 1981 the group peaked when Klecko accrued 20.5 sacks, Gastineau had 20, Salaam seven, and Lyons six. That was also the season that saw the group accept an invitation in November to ring the ceremonial opening bell at the New York Stock Exchange, further imprinting their name on the minds of the sporting public.

While they were teammates, a competition arose between Gastineau and Klecko to see which of them could record the most sacks. And there were isolated moments when Gastineau's antics performing his famed Sack Dance rubbed his teammates the wrong way.

Unfortunately for the Jets and fans of the New York Sack Exchange, they broke up the band way too soon. The group that arguably had as much talent in their front four as the Fearsome Foursome, the Purple People Eaters, and the Steel Curtain, came to an end in 1982.

Klecko suffered a knee injury and missed most of the season, NFL players went out on a 57-day strike, and, after the season, Salaam got traded by the Jets to the Chargers.

Klecko, Gastineau, and Lyons continued to play together— Klecko and Gastineau even made several Pro Bowl teams—but the group as a whole was never the same.

11 End of the Sack Dance

Toward the end of the 20th century many began to feel that *NFL* had become an acronym for the No Fun League. And any true Jets fan would be lying to say he or she felt otherwise based on the league's decision regarding Mark Gastineau's beloved Sack Dance.

In March 1984, the NFL said "no more dancing" to the stellar Jets defensive end by passing a rule that outlawed "premeditated expressions of exuberance" and would bring future offenders to justice by assessing a five-yard penalty for unsportsmanlike conduct. In part, the rule took aim at a group that played for the Washington Redskins, who called themselves the Fun Bunch after holding hands and bouncing around in the end zone after touchdowns. But clearly, shutting down Gastineau's show had been the primary intent by NFL rule-makers.

Gastineau brought a world of talent to the NFL, complete with the dance he would perform whenever he tackled the quarterback behind the line of scrimmage, thereby recording a sack. While the Sack Dance did add color, the gyrations and lack of rhythm of the performance that followed brought visions of your mom and dad dancing to the Average White Band.

Gastineau never claimed to be a dancer, but he did defend his dancing by claiming that he never danced to show up the quarterback he'd just sacked or the offensive lineman he'd beaten en route to the quarterback. Furthering that argument, Gastineau pointed out that he never performed his dance while standing next to the quarterback or an offensive lineman, rather he would shuffle off to an open area where he suddenly would become Mr. Bojangles in shoulder pads and a helmet.

Mark Gastineau goes into the Sack Dance during the AFC division playoff on January 15, 1983, where the Jets beat the Raiders 17–14. The Sack Dance was frowned on by almost everyone—opposing players, NFL brass, and even by Gastineau's own teammates.

While Gastineau maintained his innocence about the intentions of his dance, he contradicted his own words by offering a half-hearted rendition of the Sack Dance after running through Baltimore Colts tackle Jeff Hart to sack the quarterback. Gastineau told reporters that he did not care to dance much on that occasion because he did not care to show up Hart, whom he felt was one of the nicest guys in the NFL, and he respected him too much to do so.

Alas, Jackie Slater of the Los Angeles Rams did not believe in Gastineau's motives, nor did he care if he could dance like Michael Jackson, he just felt like Gastineau should not have been strutting his stuff after moving through him to sack Vince Ferragamo during a 27–24 overtime win by the Jets that took place on September 25, 1983, at Shea Stadium.

Slater brought to mind the antics of a Vaudeville stage manager giving an act the hook when he hastily moved across the field toward Gastineau and gave him a healthy shove. Marty Lyons and Kenny Neil then jumped Slater, prompting both benches to empty. The brawl that followed resulted in 37 players receiving fines that totaled $15,750, including Gastineau, who received the steepest fine of $1,000. Slater would later say that offensive linemen from around the league called to congratulate him for putting Gastineau in his place.

The Jets-Rams incident at Shea became part of the dialogue when rule-makers on the NFL's competition committee talked about ruling against Gastineau and others who might choose to express themselves on the dance floor. Miami Dolphins coach Don Shula served on the competition committee. The owners voted for the rule that came to be known as the Gastineau Rule by a vote of 26–2, which included a yea vote from the Jets. Given the fact that Gastineau had constantly had the Dolphins on his dance card, was there any wonder that the ruling went against him?

While Gastineau had to turn in his dancing shoes, Jets fans will always fondly remember the way he graced the dance floors of the NFL.

12 Don Maynard

Don Maynard earned the distinction of going from "NFL reject" status to NFL Hall of Famer.

Maynard twice earned All-Border Conference halfback honors at Texas Western College, where he also excelled at track. After his junior year, the Jets drafted him as a future in the ninth round of the 1957 draft, making him the 109th player selected.

Joining the Giants in 1958, Maynard backed up Alex Webster and Frank Gifford in the backfield and returned punts and kickoffs. But he received a lot of criticism for fumbling a punt in a game against the Cleveland Browns. Even though the Giants won that game and went on to play the Baltimore Colts for the NFL championship, Maynard wasn't a good match for the Giants, particularly as a running back.

The Giants cut Maynard the following fall, and he signed on with the Hamilton Tiger-Cats of the Canadian Football League for one season. He resurfaced in New York in 1960 with the Titans of the fledgling American Football League, becoming the first player to sign with the team that would be coached by Slingin' Sammy Baugh, who, like Maynard, also was a Texan.

Maynard's first season with the Titans, who would become the Jets, saw him catch 72 passes while combining with Art Powell to become the first receiving pair to each surpass 1,000 receiving yards in a season; they repeated the feat in 1962.

The Jets struggled for the better part of Maynard's first five seasons with the team but began to show signs of a bright future when Joe Namath joined the team in 1965. Maynard superstitiously wore No. 13, and Namath wore No. 12, so 12-to-13 became a familiar and feared passing combination.

Don Maynard, shown here in 1972, had a special relationship with Joe Namath, and the two teamed up for many stellar plays during their tenure with the Jets.

Of the 22 touchdown passes Namath threw his rookie season, 14 of them found Maynard's waiting hands. Maynard caught 68 passes in 1965 for 1,218 yards. From there, the combination continued to click, with the results seemingly getting better every year.

Maynard accounted for an AFL-leading 1,434 receiving yards on 71 catches for an average of 20.2 yards per catch with 10 going for touchdowns in 1967.

In 1968 the Jets advanced to the Super Bowl with Maynard again serving as a major cog in the team's offense by hauling in 10 touchdowns while making 57 catches for 1,297 yards.

Maynard might have put together the biggest game of his career just at the right time in the 1968 AFL Championship Game against the Oakland Raiders. The Jets took a 7–0 lead in the first quarter when he caught a 14-yard touchdown. Late in the fourth quarter with the Jets trailing 23–20, Maynard told Namath he could get open deep. He'd been setting up Raiders cornerback George

Atkinson the entire game by making a move to the inside without ever cutting back to the outside. Namath called Maynard's number, and No. 13 cut to the outside to make a 52-yard catch. He then caught a six-yard dart from Namath for the go-ahead touchdown in a 27–23 win that vaulted the Jets into Super Bowl III—and the rest is history.

When the AFL merged with the NFL, Maynard held the distinction of being one of just 20 players who had played in the AFL during its 10 years of life. He finished his NFL career when he played in two games for the St. Louis Cardinals in 1973, catching just one pass, giving him 633 receptions for 11,834 yards and 88 touchdowns for his career. In 1974 he closed out his professional career in the World Football League, catching five passes for 62 yards for the Houston Texans/Shreveport Steamer.

Maynard was selected to the Pro Football Hall of Fame and enshrined at Canton on August 8, 1987.

"Playing pro football to me was like a vacation," said Maynard in a 2004 interview. "The first five years I worked as a plumber and a teacher during the off-season. When I reported to football, I felt like I was taking a break from work."

13 Sammy Baugh

Harry Wismer's selection to become the first coach of the New York Titans—a significant choice since he would be the first coach in Jets history—was Sammy Baugh, the NFL great from the Washington Redskins.

Baugh retired from the Redskins in 1952 with virtually every passing record imaginable. Filling the air with footballs had always been Slingin' Sammy's game. Seemingly, the passing game had been invented for him.

Prior to reaching the NFL in 1937, Baugh had been a two-time All-American at Texas Christian University, which he attended only after his plans to become a baseball player were foiled when he hurt his knee sliding into a base. The injury cost him a scholarship to Washington State, but the injury turned out to be fortuitous for the youngster who had spent much of his early life practicing his passing by throwing a football through a tire hanging from a rope on a tree. TCU told him he could play three sports if he wanted, so he accepted the scholarship to join the Horned Frogs.

Baugh became a prolific passer during his college days, which included 39 touchdown passes, and he finished fourth in the Heisman Trophy voting in 1936. He also led TCU to a 3–2 win over LSU in the 1936 Sugar Bowl and led a 16–6 victory over Marquette in the first Cotton Bowl in 1937.

Professional football did not carry the glamour or the salaries that would come later in the 20th century, so making the progression to the NFL was not a foregone conclusion for any college star. The Redskins drafted Baugh in the first round with the sixth overall pick and tried to entice him into playing for the Redskins by offering him a $4,000 salary in the spring of 1937. The native Texan weighed that offer against the offer to remain at TCU as an assistant coach. Only after playing in the College All-Star Game and helping the collegians beat the Packers did Baugh decide the NFL would be for him, and he signed a one-year deal for $8,000, thereby making him the Redskins' highest-paid player.

Baugh would more than prove his worth. By the time he retired after the 1952 season, Baugh had 13 NFL records to his name, which included his work as a quarterback, punter, and defensive back. Though he did not invent the forward pass, Baugh is credited with being the first quarterback to truly put the pass to work.

Shortly after retiring, Baugh became an assistant coach at Hardin-Simmon University in Texas, which led to his becoming the school's head football coach in 1955. In five seasons his teams compiled an unimpressive 23–28 record. Wismer, who was the founder of the Titans and had a relationship with Baugh from his days as the radio broadcaster and part owner of the Redskins, hired Baugh in December 1959 to become the team's first coach prior to the American Football League's first season.

Baugh brought his Texas manner and wide-open style of football to New York, which fit in perfectly with the exciting brand of football desired by the fledgling league. He served two seasons as the team's coach, leaving the Titans after the 1961 season with a 14–14 record.

Baugh went on to become an assistant coach at the University of Tulsa before returning to the AFL in 1964 as the coach of the Houston Oilers, leading the team to a 4–10 mark.

In 1963 Baugh was inducted into the Pro Football Hall of Fame as part of the inaugural class that included Red Grange, Don Hutson, Bronko Nagurski, Curly Lambeau, Jim Thorpe, Ernie Nevers, George Halas, and Mel Hein.

14 Remember the Titans

The American Football League held a meeting in Chicago on August 14, 1959, in which charter franchises for the fledgling league were granted to Los Angeles, Dallas, Minneapolis, Houston, Denver, and New York.

And just like that, New York had the Titans, a second professional football team.

Larry Grantham

By the end of the 1972 season, the Jets had two players still on the team from the original 1960 Titans squad: wide receiver Don Maynard and linebacker Larry Grantham.

By the beginning of the next season, only Maynard remained, as Grantham retired in July 1973. In leaving, the 6'0", 210-pound linebacker from Ole Miss left a legacy of hard-nosed football and heart. Opposing quarterbacks always knew who played the left outside linebacker spot for the Jets because Grantham made his presence known; he always finished among the top tacklers in the league.

Grantham played during an era when the play-calling on offense belonged to the quarterback, and on defense it belonged to the linebacker. Grantham was that man for the Jets.

"Larry knew what everybody on defense was supposed to do on every play," Paul Rochester told the *New York Times*. Rochester played defensive left tackle on the Jets team that beat the Baltimore Colts 16–7 in Super Bowl III. "The Colts kept running at me and Gerry Philbin, so Larry kept calling the same defense. 'They're coming your way,' he'd yell. 'Just keep stopping 'em.'"

When Grantham retired at the age of 34, he brought to a close a career that ran from 1960, when the Jets were the Titans, to 1972, when the Jets were a member of the NFL and had a Super Bowl win under their belts.

Grantham had intended to play football just two years when he began his career in 1960.

"I just could never get around to quitting," Grantham said upon his retirement.

When Grantham left, just four original members of the AFL remained active. They were Maynard; George Blanda, quarterback/kicker for the Oakland Raiders; Jim Otto, Raiders center; and Ernie Wright, an offensive tackle for the San Diego Chargers.

Grantham was named to the AFL All-Star team five times and played in eight league All-Star Games; in addition, he was selected to the All-Time All-AFL second team. Grantham was also named the 1971 New York Jets MVP.

Grantham remains part of a unique fraternity as one of only 20 players who were in the AFL for all 10 years of its existence.

Soon the chaos began to sort itself out—as did the cities where the teams would play— and the Titans found themselves grouped in the East division along with Boston, Buffalo, and Houston, while Oakland, Dallas, Denver, and Los Angeles were set up to compose the West.

Colorful Harry Wismer was the founder and owner of the team—named after the nation's largest missile—and secured use of New York's famed Polo Grounds to serve as the team's home field. NFL great and future Hall of Famer Sammy Baugh was Wismer's selection to become the Titans' first coach for an annual salary of $28,000.

The Titans participated in the first AFL Draft on November 22, 1959. Thirty-three rounds took place on the first day, followed by an additional 20 rounds 10 days later. Typical of a franchise that would grow to believe that it carried a curse on Draft Day, the Titans selected Notre Dame quarterback George Izo with their first overall pick only to see him sign with the NFL's St. Louis Cardinals.

Draft Day futility aside, the Titans did manage to find and sign Don Maynard as the first Titans player. Maynard had begun his professional career with the New York Giants before leaving the NFL for the Canadian Football League. The Maynard signing turned out to be a pretty savvy move, as the flanker would become one of the best players in franchise history en route to becoming a Hall of Famer.

Baugh, colorful and unflappable, served as the perfect coach for a new team trying to compete against the likes of the Giants. Even the caliber of his team's talent could not diminish Baugh's spirits when he spoke of his team.

"We're going to have a real team," Baugh told the *New York Times*. "We'll start training up in New Hampshire with about 70 boys, none of whose names, probably, are known to the general public. But what's in a name? Give me boys like we have signed, most of them 200 pounds and over and most of them quick, and

I'll have a football team. Steve Sebo, our general manager, who's been coaching some himself and knows talent when he sees it, informs me, for instance, that we will have nine outstanding quarterback prospects. He has an imposing list of halfbacks, fullbacks, and linemen, too. I don't mean to give the impression that the Titans, in their first year, will be the greatest football team ever organized. We'll have to build and experiment and change. But we'll have a football team at the start that'll be worth watching."

Initially, the masses felt otherwise.

The Titans played their first game on September 11, 1960, wearing the team's colors of blue and gold. Attendance proved disappointing—the Titans drew just 9,607, which was a reflection of the players playing in the game, most of whom were NFL castoffs and Canadian League veterans. After the Titans' first game, Titans tackle Sid Youngelman, who played six seasons in the NFL, told *Sport Illustrated*, "In the NFL there are no weak spots. Here, while you don't relax, you are better able to pace yourself." The Titans did not draw well for several years, but they managed to survive. They became the Jets in 1963, and the rest is history.

15 Mark Gastineau

Mark Gastineau arrived in the NFL as a freak because, prior to his arrival, nobody had seen a player of his ilk. He would become a prototype for future pass-rushers, becoming one of the best players in Jets history and certainly one of the more colorful.

Not only did Gastineau have size—at 6'5" and 266 pounds— and speed, he was an athlete, and he did the necessary work in the

Four Sacks for Abraham

Shortly after being selected by the Jets in the first round of the 2000 NFL Draft with the 13th overall pick, John Abraham got off on the wrong foot with the team's fans when he spoke about wanting to make a difference—for the New York Giants.

Once the 6'4", 256-pound defensive end from South Carolina figured out he would be playing for the Jets instead of the Giants, he did in fact make a difference. But nothing Abraham did would surpass what he accomplished in New Orleans on November 4, 2001.

The Jets entered the game with a 4–3 record hoping to keep what had been a winning season intact under new coach Herm Edwards, a former NFL defensive back who preached defense. Only in his second season with the Jets, Abraham had already developed into an impact player, giving the Saints exactly what they wanted, a defensive end who could put pressure on the quarterback.

New Orleans entered the game with a 4–2 mark thanks in large part to their fleet-footed quarterback, Aaron Brooks, who could scramble around in the pocket to avoid even the best of pass rushers. Figuring into the equation for the contest was the fact that Willie Roaf, the Saints' All-Pro tackle, could not play. And Abraham was more than happy to exploit his absence by recording four sacks for the game, jerking down Brooks on fourth down at the Saints' 20 on the final play of the game for his final sack.

By collecting four sacks in one game, Abraham tied the club record held by Mark Lomas, who achieved the feat once, and Mark Gastineau, who turned the trick three times.

Abraham finished the 2001 season with 13 sacks, and the Jets went 10–6 to earn a spot in the playoffs, where they lost in the opening round.

Unfortunately for Abraham and the Jets, that would become Abraham's best season with the team.

Abraham had 10 sacks in 2002 and 10½ in 2005, but he battled injuries during the 2003 and 2004 seasons, which limited his playing time. The Jets traded him to the Falcons after the 2005 season, and he promptly set a franchise record with 16½ sacks.

weight room to better prepare himself for battle in the NFL trenches.

Gastineau became a Junior College All-American selection at Eastern Arizona Junior College before heading to Arizona State, where he dropped out. He ended up at East Central University in Ada, Oklahoma, a school that had never produced an NFL player.

Despite the relative obscurity of the school, Gastineau played well enough to earn a spot on the North team in the 1979 Senior Bowl. To that point, NFL scouts projected Gastineau to be a latter-round pick. But once they got to see him compete with the players from the "bigger" colleges, they grew smitten with his physicality and his 4.8 speed in the 40-yard dash. More than anyone, Gastineau understood that his speed would define him.

The Jets' coaching staff had coached the North team in the Senior Bowl and grew so smitten with his ability that they selected him in the second round of the 1979 draft. Once on the Jets, he continued to work to refine his speed until he could run an unheard-of time of 4.56 in the 40. Defensive linemen were simply not supposed to be so fast.

By Gastineau's second season, in 1980, he began to put his many physical gifts on display when he posted a team-leading 11.5 sacks. Jets fans also got a hint of things to come when he began to dance after some of his sacks. Opponents did not like Gastineau's gyrations, which resembled a wounded duck. Gastineau's teammates did not like the dancing either. Given the fact Gastineau did not feel well liked by his teammates, he made the decision to dance after every sack.

Gastineau earned first-team All-Pro honors in 1982, 1983, 1984, and 1985 and was voted the NFL's Defensive Player of the Year in 1982. Gastineau first led the NFL in sacks in 1983 when he recorded 19. The following year he won the UPI AFC Defensive Player of the Year honors when he had a record-setting 22 sacks (a record broken in 2001 by Michael Strahan of the New York Giants when he had 22.5 sacks).

Throughout it all, Gastineau remained a high-profile figure who always seemed to have an interesting twist just around the corner. He trained to become a professional boxer during the 1982 NFL players' strike, he lifted weights more like a bodybuilder than a football player, and he maintained a highly visible romance with actress Brigitte Nielsen.

When Nielsen had health problems in 1988, Gastineau retired, citing a desire to spend more time with her during her trying time, and he remained retired until playing four games for the BC Lions of the Canadian Football League in 1990.

After retiring from football, Gastineau experienced many personal problems and troubles with the law—which included an 11-month stint in prison in 1999 for parole violations.

Gastineau's problems in the days following his football career have dimmed his accomplishments and made him an unlikely candidate to get into the Hall of Fame. Problems aside, Gastineau always will be remembered for his antics, his ability, and his status as one of the best players in team history.

Harry Wismer

Colorful, flamboyant, and *eccentric* were just some of the words used to describe the founder and first owner of the New York Titans, the team that would become the Jets.

Wismer grew up loving sports, participating in them and following them during the early years of his life, which led to his becoming a three-sport letterman at St. John's Military Academy in Delafield, Wisconsin. Of the three, football prevailed, and Wismer would go on to play at the University of Florida and Michigan State before injuring his knee and making an easy transition into the broadcast booth for Michigan State sports.

Wismer parlayed his job broadcasting Spartans sports into a gig as the public-address announcer for the NFL's Detroit Lions, which enabled him to meet George A. "Dick" Richards, the Lions' owner as well as the owner of a Detroit radio station, WJR.

Still a student at Michigan State, Wismer's job with the Lions blossomed into a position with WJR as the station's sports director, and he opted to leave Michigan State before graduating. While he didn't have his diploma, Wismer had already attained a belief system about what it took to succeed: relationships.

Wismer embraced the philosophy that it wasn't what you knew, rather it was all about *who* you knew. He would successfully ride that philosophy for the rest of his life.

Wismer evolved into a freelance broadcaster and found great success in the endeavor, eventually landing in the role where he attained his highest visibility, as the voice of the Washington Redskins. A slaughter marked Wismer's debut for the Redskins as he called the 1940 NFL Championship Game that saw the Chicago Bears destroy the Redskins 73–0.

Having found his way into the Redskins family, Wismer worked up to a point where he became a 25 percent owner of the club, which George Preston Marshall owned. Later the pair had a falling out over a social issue that came down to Wismer not agreeing with Marshall's reluctance to sign black players. This led to Wismer leaving the Redskins and divesting himself of his Redskins stock.

Wismer continued to be a pioneer in broadcasting, working for ABC in 1953 broadcasting replays of Notre Dame football games on Sundays following the Saturday games.

The 1953 season also found Wismer helping with the DuMont Network's attempt at broadcasting NFL games in prime time, which was presented live on Saturday nights. Both ventures were well ahead of their time but did not work out.

Nevertheless, Wismer became a well-known broadcaster and managed to become a wealthy man along the way, and that helped him bankroll his interest in having a team in the newly created American Football League.

As owner of the Titans, Wismer did all he could to try and make the team and the league a success. Seeing Wismer walking into different businesses around Manhattan promoting the Titans became a common sight. Wismer helped the AFL to no end by understanding that while his team played in the most attractive market in the league, it needed successful teams to play in order to find success. Thus, he created a plan that allowed broadcast rights from the games to be shared equally by all of the teams.

Wismer is also remembered for having celebrated feuds with Titans coach and NFL legend Sammy Baugh, AFL commissioner Joe Foss, and the other AFL owners.

Unfortunately for Wismer, he did not have the money to continue backing a team that drew just 114,682 total paid admissions for the team's first season and saw that number drop to 36,161 in 1962. In February 1963, Wismer sold the team for $1 million to the Gotham Football Club, which was headed by Sonny Werblin, who had deep financial pockets. Under Werblin, the team relocated to Shea Stadium, a far better venue than the Polo Grounds, and changed its name to the Jets.

When Wismer left the AFL, he was debt-riddled. On December 2, 1967, Wismer fell down a flight of steps and died the next day at the age of 56.

17 Weeb Ewbank

When Weeb Ewbank took over the reins as head coach of the New York Jets in 1963, he had already coached the winning team in the game many judged the biggest in NFL history.

By the time his tenure with the Jets had run its course, Ewbank had coached in the two top games in the history of the National Football League and won both.

In 1958 Ewbank served as the Baltimore Colts' coach when they played the New York Giants in the 1958 NFL Championship Game and came away with a 23–17 win in what has been referred to as "the greatest game ever played."

During his nine-year tenure with the Colts, Ewbank took the team from obscurity to two-time NFL champions—they repeated by defeating the Giants in the 1959 NFL Championship Game. The fact alone that Ewbank's Colts defeated the Giants twice in the big game would have eternally endeared him to Jets fans, but bigger things were ahead, much bigger things.

After the Colts went 7–7 in 1962, team owner Carroll Rosenbloom fired Ewbank in favor of Don Shula, thereby opening the door for Jets owner Sonny Werblin to hire him to coach the team beginning in 1963, a move that coincided with a change of the team's name and colors. The Titans were moving to sparkling new Shea Stadium in 1964, which was near LaGuardia Airport. Based on that proximity, *Jets* felt like a perfect name for the team, so they quit being the Titans and became the Jets in 1963. Upon taking over the Jets, who had been anything but a stellar American Football League franchise, Ewbank optimistically told reporters, "I've seen sicker cows than this get well."

Quarterback Joe Namath with his father (right) and Jets coach Weeb Ewbank after the Jets triumphed 16–7 over the Colts in Super Bowl III.

Hiring Ewbank added instant credibility to the Jets and the AFL.

"Weeb was a real coach," said former Jets wide receiver Don Maynard in a Yahoo! Sports article. "When the AFL first got started, the writers used to knock it all the time, saying it was filled with ex-NFL guys who couldn't make it over there. Then Werblin comes in, brings Weeb over and all of a sudden, the news media started to take us seriously. It got to be fun."

45

Ewbank had a unique talent for assessing his players and would often move them to positions better suiting their abilities. He also left the players alone away from the field, believing that what they did on the field was their responsibility, and what they did away from the football field was their business.

Ewbank coached the Jets when they lost the famed Heidi Bowl, which led to a humorous story. In that game, the Jets lost 43–32 to the Raiders after NBC cut away from their telecast of the game with 65 seconds left—and the Jets winning 32–29—to show the movie *Heidi*. Characteristic of Ewbank was the story of what happened after the game when his wife, Lucy, called to congratulate him.

Ewbank asked his wife, "For what?"

Lucy then told him she was congratulating him for winning the game, to which Ewbank famously replied, "We lost the game."

Ewbank had a roly-poly look to him, packaged on a 5'7", 195-pound frame that belied the coach behind the appearance. Initially even Joe Namath mocked his coach's appearance. Ewbank won over his marquee quarterback with his football intelligence and coaching acumen. By the time the Jets reached Super Bowl III against Ewbank's former team, the Colts, Namath had bought into his coach, who had earned Namath's total respect.

Prior to that epic contest, Ewbank told his team dirty jokes to keep the mood light, and he even spun a yarn about having a bad leg, noting that they would need to be gentle when they carried him off the field after they had beaten the Colts.

Whether or not the players handled Ewbank gently is unknown, but they did go out and pull off what is considered the greatest upset in NFL history by defeating the Colts 16–7.

While the game appeared to be Ewbank's finest day in terms of exacting revenge on the team that had fired him, he never gloated about the win. Over the years he would encapsulate the gist of the game by telling people that the Jets had played well that day in

Top-Notch Assistants

Head coaches get the credit when a team does well and the blame when they don't. But the true fates of many are due to whom they have backing them as assistant coaches.

While the Jets have won just one Super Bowl, they have had their share of top-notch assistants, beginning with the coach who is believed to be the NFL's best since Bill Parcells retired, Bill Belichick.

Belichick, a Parcells disciple, served as the assistant head coach/defensive coordinator under Parcells from 1997 to 1999 and had initially agreed to become Parcells' successor as the head coach of the Jets but changed his mind to take over the New England Patriots.

Bud Carson coached the Jets' defense from 1985 to 1988 after achieving fame as the Pittsburgh Steelers' defensive coordinator for the Steel Curtain defense. Under Carson, the Steelers became one of the best defenses in NFL history.

Chuck Knox served as the Jets' offensive-line coach under head coach Weeb Ewbank for four years. He is credited with building the offensive line that would protect the Jets' most prized asset, Joe Namath.

Knox went on to become a two-time coach of the Los Angeles Rams, the Seattle Seahawks, and the Buffalo Bills.

Dan Henning served as an assistant for the Jets from 1976 to 1978 and most recently as the quarterbacks coach from 1998 to 2000. Henning established a track record as an offensive mastermind, having his biggest success while being the offensive coordinator for two Super Bowl–winning teams with the Washington Redskins. He also served as the head coach for the San Diego Chargers and Atlanta Falcons and had a stint as the head coach of Boston College.

Sam Rutigliano served as an assistant for the Jets from 1974 to 1975 in advance of becoming the head coach of the Cleveland Browns in 1978. He went on to become the NFL Coach of the Year in 1980.

Ken Whisenhunt was an assistant for the Jets in 2000 before earning his bones with the Steelers, where he worked his way up from tight-ends coach to offensive coordinator. He took over as the head coach of the Arizona Cardinals in 2007 and led the team to the Super Bowl following the 2008 season.

Miami and that they had gotten all the breaks. In other words, Ewbank personified class.

Ewbank coached the Jets for 11 seasons to finish his professional coaching career with a 134–130 record that included seven ties. The results don't look earth-shattering, but considering the fact that he successfully conducted building operations with the Colts and Jets that culminated in championships, it's little wonder he was inducted into the Pro Football Hall of Fame in 1998.

Ironically, Ewbank died at the age of 91, on November 17, 1998, the 30th anniversary of the Heidi Bowl.

18 First Game in Franchise History

Jets players were dressed in blue and gold when the team played its first game on September 11, 1960, as the New York Titans.

Under coach Sammy Baugh, the Titans began their first training camp in July, then suffered through four consecutive losses in exhibition games before finishing their preseason slate with a 52–31 win over the Bills. Throughout the preseason, Baugh had experimented with the team's offense, looking to move his team toward a wide-open attack, which meant filling the air with footballs. And the Titans appeared to be drawing near where the former NFL great wanted his team to be, given the nature of the win over the Bills.

The Titans were in the American Football League's Eastern Division along with the Boston Patriots, Houston Oilers, and Buffalo Bills, and the experts figured they were the worst of the bunch.

Two former NFL quarterbacks of little note were expected to call the signals for the Titans in their regular-season opener against the Bills: Dick Jamieson and Al Dorow.

Jamieson had been on the Baltimore Colts' taxi squad the previous season. A lot was made of the fact that Jamieson had been around Johnny Unitas while with the Colts, and any exposure to the man heralded as the best quarterback in the game had to be good.

Meanwhile, Dorow had spent time with the Washington Redskins and Philadelphia Eagles.

If they were indeed going to be successful running the type of offense Baugh favored, the Titans needed quality receivers for Jamieson and Dorow to throw to, and the team got lucky by bringing former NFL receivers Art Powell, Thurlow Cooper, and Don Maynard into the fold.

Titans home games were scheduled to be played at the Polo Grounds, site of so many great moments in Major League Baseball, but the field did not meet the standards demanded by Titans owner Harry Wismer when he inspected the turf on Friday, two days before the Titans' Sunday opener.

Wismer had a contract with the National Exhibition Company, which managed the field at the Polo Grounds, and the contract specified that the field be in mint condition for the Titans following the close of a soccer league that had used the Polo Grounds. Despite the contract, the field needed a lot of work. Wismer's inspection revealed holes, ruts, and exposed drainage covers, which forced him to hire a sizeable work crew that worked on Friday and Saturday to get the field into proper condition by Sunday afternoon.

The Titans expected a crowd of 20,000 to see the opener. They were not the first team to take the field in the fledgling eight-team American Football League, as the Boston Patriots had already played the Denver Broncos on Friday, September 9, and the Dallas Texans had played the Los Angeles Chargers on Saturday night.

Meanwhile, coinciding with the Titans game was an exhibition game between the New York Giants and Detroit Lions at the Yale

Bowl in New Hartford, Connecticut, where the crowd was anticipated to be in the neighborhood of 55,000.

Further bad news for the Titans came in the weather for the
opener. Rain soaked the field, which loosened the newly laid sod
and led to muddy playing conditions. A crowd of 9,607 showed to
watch the game, of which just 5,727 were paying customers.

After Jamieson had trouble getting anything started for the
Titans, Dorow came off the bench in the second quarter with the
score tied at 3.

The Bills had a poor punt and gave the Titans the ball at the
Bills' 43 to set up the Titans' first score. Hoping to take advantage
of the field position, Dorow lofted a pass that Maynard hauled in
with a leaping grab at the 20. From there the drive advanced to the
Bills' 4, setting up a run around the left end by Dorow, who went
into the end zone untouched, thanks to an eye-opening block by
Maynard.

Later in the quarter, Dorow raced around right end for a 15-
yard touchdown. Jamieson connected on a 15-yard touchdown pass
to Powell with 18 seconds remaining to close out the scoring.

Final score: Titans 27, Bills 3.

And the team that would become the New York Jets had its first
win in franchise history.

19 Grow a Fu Manchu

At the risk of looking like a pool boy in a movie starring Ron
Jeremy, any true male Jets fan must at some point grow a Fu
Manchu moustache to pay homage to the greatest Jet ever, Joe
Namath.

Suzy Kolber and Broadway Joe

Joe Namath experienced a public embarrassment on December 20, 2003, but in this case, everything was self-inflicted for the former Jets great.

During halftime of a Jets game against the New England Patriots, Namath had been honored as part of a newly elected all-time team and apparently had enjoyed a little too much champagne celebrating the honor.

ESPN aired the game, which led to Suzy Kolber conducting an interview with Namath, and she asked the Jets great about watching his former team go through hard times that season.

Namath answered Kolber's question by telling her, "I want to kiss you. I couldn't care less about the team struggling. What we know is we can improve. Chad Pennington, our quarterback, missed the first part of the season, and we struggled. We're looking to next season. We're looking to make noise now, and I want to kiss you."

If those comments weren't enough, Broadway Joe finished off his remarks with an enthusiastic, "Yeah!"

Kolber kept her cool and told him, "Thanks, Joe, I'll take that as a huge compliment."

Joe Theismann and Paul Maguire were analysts for the telecast, and each had a little something to say about Namath's highly irrational behavior.

Theismann said to his TV audience, "Joe is just a happy guy."

Maguire added, "Oh boy, is he happy."

In the days that followed, Namath apologized to Kolber. Weeks later, he told ESPN during an interview, "I can't believe it, and I didn't even see it, and I don't want to see it. That was the wake-up call. Even before that, I said, 'Yeah, I'm going to stop, I'm going to stop.' I stopped, and, like I say, I stopped for a few weeks, I stopped for a week, I stopped for two weeks, and then go back and drink a couple of days. Not constantly, just a couple, few drinks. I can't handle it."

Namath entered an outpatient alcoholism treatment program. The day he began treatment was January 12, 2004, the 35th anniversary of Super Bowl III.

Mark Sanchez obviously understands the man and the moustache because he has already fashioned a Fu Manchu to pay his respects toward Namath. So is it too much to ask of a Jets fan to let one grow just as Namath once did?

During the Jets' 1968 drive toward the Super Bowl, facial hair became the rage for many of the Jets players. The idea was to keep the facial hair alive until they reached the American Football League Championship Game. Despite the fact that many of the players took part in the hirsute theme, only one received attention for doing so. Of course, Namath was the guy.

Even if everybody else had a moustache, goatee, or any variety of facial fashions, Namath had the Fu Manchu, making the moustache either sinister or cool depending on which side of the fence you stood when viewing the hip Namath, who enjoyed nothing better than bucking the system.

Namath sported the Fu Manchu for approximately two months, and the moustache seemed to take on a personality of its own. Photographs of Namath and his suddenly trademark moustache appeared everywhere. He even adorned the cover of *Sports Illustrated* with a bold photo of his moustachioed face, further perpetuating his renegade image.

While wearing the facial hair, the Jets managed to reach their goal of making the AFL Championship Game by winning the Eastern Division, which prompted several players to shave, but not without first putting a little money in their pockets. Jim Hudson, Cornell Gordon, and Bake Turner each received $250 from Remington razors for shaving their facial hair during a ceremony. The money might not sound like much, but consider the fact that tickets for the AFL Championship Game were going for $5. Which made the money Namath got for shaving his moustache seem preposterous.

Schick wrote a check to Namath for a reported fee of $10,000 to shave his Fu Manchu for a TV commercial. One New York stylist estimated that the average Fu Manchu had approximately a thousand hairs. Doing the math, that came down to $10 per hair for shaving the moustache. Not bad money considering men wake every day dreading the morning ritual that they perform for free.

Namath went to a studio on East 78th Street on December 11, 1968, to introduce his Fu Manchu to a Schick razor with three cameras recording the action and three models around him to coo over his razor work. Looking fashionable as usual, Namath wore a blue sports coat, a blue turtleneck, and blue bell-bottomed slacks.

Later that afternoon, Namath went to practice at Shea Stadium, and his teammates teased their newly shorn quarterback.

The Jets had played well during Namath's Fu Manchu phase, so as athletes there were superstitious concerns about how he would play without it. Nevertheless, Namath played pretty well without his Fu Manchu in both the AFL Championship Game and in the Super Bowl.

20 Visit Jets Hall of Famers in Canton

The Pro Football Hall of Fame is located in Canton, Ohio, which makes for an ideal trip for any Jets fan to see the main Jets contingent: Weeb Ewbank, who was enshrined in 1978, Don Maynard (1987), Joe Namath (1985), and John Riggins (1992).

The Pro Football Hall of Fame opened in 1963 and, ironically, Sammy Baugh, the first coach in Jets history—Titans at the time—was part of the inaugural class. Since that modest beginning in a 19,000-square-foot museum, everything about the Hall of Fame has grown, from the size of the facility to its grand stature.

Lott and Monk

By the time Ronnie Lott and Art Monk arrived on the Jets, the body of work for each of their Hall of Fame careers had been done. But while playing for the Jets, both had enough left in the tank to show what had made them Hall of Fame players.

Lott was an All-American safety at USC before playing for the San Francisco 49ers from 1981 to 1990 and the Oakland Raiders from 1991 to 1992.

Lott started 31 games for the Jets during the 1993 and 1994 seasons and made the final three interceptions of his career in a Jets uniform, giving him 63 in 14 NFL seasons.

During his career, Lott garnished 10 Pro Bowl invitations, made first-team All-Pro six seasons, had five 100-tackle seasons, and earned four Super Bowl rings with San Francisco. He made 20 playoff starts in which he picked off nine passes, made 89 tackles, and scored two touchdowns.

Lott was named to the NFL's 75th Anniversary Team and was inducted into the Hall of Fame in 2000. When Lott entered the Hall of Fame, he became the first former Jets player to play defense and make it to Canton.

Monk began his NFL career in 1980 after the Washington Redskins made the Syracuse receiver their first-round pick of the 1980 NFL Draft, 18th overall.

Monk stood 6'3" and weighed 210 pounds, giving the Redskins a big target for 14 seasons, and he thrived, catching 888 passes in 205 games, helping the Redskins win three Super Bowls.

Monk joined the Jets in 1994 and played one season with the Gang Green, where he served as a backup to Rob Moore and Johnny Mitchell. He caught at least one pass in every game that season, finishing the year with 46 catches for 581 yards and three touchdowns. Memorable among his catches was the five-yard pass he caught from Boomer Esiason on December 10, 1994, when the Jets played the Detroit Lions. The catch moved Monk past Steve Largent to establish an NFL-record 178th consecutive game with a reception.

Monk finished his career in 1995 with the Philadelphia Eagles. He left the game with five 1,000-yard seasons under his belt, two All-Pro selections, and three Pro Bowl berths. In 2008 he was inducted into the Hall of Fame.

Today the Hall of Fame museum is housed in an 83,000-square-foot building that has become a tourist destination for those wanting to see the story of the game everyone loves and the tributes within to those who made professional football the top sport in the United States.

Canton was chosen as the location for the Hall of Fame because the American Professional Football Association, which became the NFL, was founded in Canton on September 17, 1920. Other enticements were the fact that Jim Thorpe, remembered as the greatest athlete of the early 20th century, played his first pro football with the Canton Bulldogs, one of the early pro football powerhouses.

Upon entering the building, visitors will initially be struck by the seven-foot bronze statue of Thorpe that greets them. They will then move to the second floor, where a quick education is provided about the first century of pro football. From there the next stage is the Teams of the NFL Exhibition Area. Jets fans can find a tribute to the Jets, as each of the NFL's 32 teams are represented.

The Jets greats enshrined there can be found in the Hall of Fame Gallery, where there are bronze busts of each inductee, meaning a Jets fan can pay proper homage to Ewbank, Riggins, Namath, and Maynard. A nice feature of the area provides visitors an opportunity to learn more about those enshrined with touch-screen kiosks that include bios, photos, and video of the inductees.

Also holding significance is the Moments, Memories & Momentos Gallery that focuses on the achievements of the members of the Hall of Fame using high-tech video, audio, and lighting, which are all used to help bring to life some of the many artifacts.

Jets fans won't want to miss the Super Bowl Room, which recaps all of the Super Bowls played to date and displays memorabilia from those games as well. Yes, there are plenty of reminders that the Jets—not the Baltimore Colts—won Super Bowl III.

And don't worry about finding something to commemorate your visit, because the Hall of Fame's gift shop has many interesting products, including something for all of the 32 teams, along with unique Hall of Fame products. These products are also available online at www.profootballhof.com/store.

The Hall of Fame is located in the northwest corner of Canton, just off Interstate 77. Canton, Ohio, is located approximately 50 miles south of Cleveland, 100 miles west of Pittsburgh, and 120 miles northeast of Columbus. The Hall of Fame is open every day (except Christmas) from 9:00 AM until 5:00 PM and has extended summer hours from Memorial Day through Labor Day.

21 Watch *Beaver Falls: Where Is Joe Namath?*

Joe Namath remains the most highly celebrated citizen to ever come from Beaver Falls, Pennsylvania, yet there is really no tribute to Namath in the city located 28 miles from Pittsburgh.

This is the premise of a must-see film for Jets fans titled, *Beaver Falls: Where Is Joe Namath?*

When Namath came into the world on May 31, 1943, Beaver Falls was known as a steel-mill town. Of course, this was back when all of Pennsylvania consisted of steel towns. Friends called Namath "Joe Willie" in the city that was boxed in by a river on one side and railroad tracks on two other sides. A kid could walk to school every day, and Namath's life was simple. He played baseball, basketball, and football and earned his money by caddying at a local golf course and working at an assortment of other jobs.

Namath never realized how small Beaver Falls was while he lived there, but by the time he reached his senior year at Beaver Falls High School, he had the itch to do more, which is a familiar itch for many 18-year-olds.

By then, Namath starred in every sport and was even said to have been offered a $50,000 bonus to sign with the Chicago Cubs. Instead, he opted for football, which lead him to Tuscaloosa, Alabama, where he played for legendary coach Paul "Bear" Bryant.

While Namath would attend Alabama in advance of heading to New York to play for the Jets, and he loved living in the big city and the privileges of being a celebrity in that city, he never forgot home. Namath forever credited Beaver Falls for helping him to become the person he became and for establishing his values, his viewpoints, and how he treated people. The blue-collar environment in Beaver Falls taught him about hard work and earning whatever you got in life.

Namath grew up in the Lower End area of Beaver Falls, so most of his neighbors were African American. That upbringing helped him learn to respect everybody and treat them accordingly. He would even defend African Americans in arguments with teammates at the University of Alabama, which had not yet been integrated.

In essence, Beaver Falls meant a lot to Namath, and he never forgot where he came from, nor did he ever take pot shots at his hometown, no matter how small-town or podunk Beaver Falls seemed to others.

Beaver Falls: Where Is Joe Namath? was Dan Woodske's debut film, and it examines several issues concerning the city that experienced a difficult time adjusting to the demise of the steel industry. Among those issues is the fact that the city has never done anything to honor Namath and, therefore, actually missed an opportunity to capitalize on his fame.

The film is more than just a look at a small town not recognizing its local hero. Rather the film serves as a microcosm for Small Town, USA, and Jets fans, after watching the film, will have a deeper insight into Namath and why he became who he did.

22 Curtis Martin

Curtis Martin will likely go down as one of the most unheralded players in NFL history, but he was a special player and one Jets fans won't soon forget.

Martin's entry into the NFL came when the New England Patriots drafted him in the third round out of the University of Pittsburgh and he immediately thrived, running for 1,487 yards in his 1995 rookie season, earning Offensive Rookie of the Year and Pro Bowl honors.

During Martin's second season, the Patriots made the playoffs and he set a club record by rushing for 166 yards and three touchdowns in his first playoff game to lead a Patriots win over the Steelers. In addition, the Patriots went to the Super Bowl that season, where they lost to the Green Bay Packers.

Martin cracked the 1,000-yard plateau again in his second and third seasons with the Patriots, but for some inexplicable reason, they allowed him to slip away.

Jets coach Bill Parcells, who had coached Martin in New England, recognized Martin's rare talents. So when Martin became a restricted free agent after the 1997 season, Parcells and the Jets signed him to an offer sheet for $36 million to play for the Jets for six years. The Patriots did not match the Jets' offer. The Patriots received compensation in the way of first- and third-round draft picks, but draft picks were nothing compared to what Martin brought to the Jets.

Martin brought an unheard-of toughness to the Jets' running-back position, missing just one game in his first seven seasons with the team. Among the highlights from this steady offensive force was the 1998 playoff game against the Jacksonville Jaguars that saw him gain 182 yards rushing in the Jets' win.

In his first 10 seasons in the NFL, Martin surpassed 1,000 yards rushing, and he became the oldest player in NFL history to lead the league in rushing in 2004 when he ran for 1,697. Martin had a chance to become the first player in NFL history to rush for 1,000 yards in his first 11 seasons but missed the final four games of the 2005 season with a knee injury and finished the season with 735 yards rushing. The bone-on-bone condition in his right knee that caused him to miss the remainder of the 2005 season eventually led to him announcing his retirement on July 26, 2007.

When Martin retired, NFL commissioner Roger Goodell said in a statement, "Curtis Martin represents everything an NFL player should be. He overcame many challenges to enjoy an outstanding career as one of the best running backs in the NFL. His on-field accomplishments were matched by an equally strong commitment to serving his community and being a positive role model off the field. We know that Curtis will continue to be successful and represent the NFL well as he moves into his next career."

Martin finished with 14,101 career yards on 3,518 carries, scored 100 touchdowns, and had 57 regular-season 100-yard rushing games.

At his retirement news conference, Martin told the media, "I don't see this as a sad time. The best moment of my career is right now. I don't have any regrets. I'm leaving the game just the way I'd like to."

23 John Riggins

John Riggins is remembered for a lot of things he did as a member of the Jets. For a while he fashioned an Afro, and at another juncture he wore a Mohawk. He never shied away from saying what was on his mind. And, foremost, he was a football player.

Riggins came to the Jets in 1971 after being selected in the first round with the sixth pick of the NFL Draft out of the University of Kansas, where he broke Gayle Sayers' career rushing mark. A bruising bull of a fullback, Riggins had size—230 pounds—speed, and the necessary toughness to make an immediate impact.

Nicknamed "the Diesel," Riggins showed all of the above as he bulldozed his way to 769 yards on 180 carries in his rookie season. In his second season, Riggins carried the ball 207 times and gained 944 yards despite missing the final two games due to knee surgery. Unfortunately for the Jets, the 1972 season would be the season that soured him on the Jets and left him disillusioned about the game for several years.

Weeb Ewbank coached the Jets and served as the team's general manager, much to Riggins' chagrin.

The Kansas native understood why Ewbank lowballed him on his first contract with the Jets since he had not accomplished anything in the NFL. But when the time came for Riggins to sign his contract for the 1973 season, Ewbank chastised him for not reaching the 1,000-yard plateau. After that, Riggins lost his joy for the game while growing an understanding that professional football was a business.

Riggins got even with the Jets when he played out his option during the 1975 season. To do so, he had to take a 10 percent pay

John Riggins sports some killer hair in 1972.

cut from his 1974 salary, but he no longer wanted to play for the Jets, so he felt the loss of pay to be worthwhile.

Riggins went out and put together his best season as a Jet in his final season with the team in 1975 by rushing the football 238 times for 1,005 yards—the first time he surpassed the magical barrier for running backs, and he scored eight touchdowns.

In May 1976 Riggins was granted free-agent status and eventually signed with the Redskins, which is where he played until his retirement following the 1985 season.

Riggins finished his career with 11,352 yards and 116 touchdowns. He is probably best remembered for his touchdown jaunt in Super Bowl XVII when the Redskins played the Dolphins.

The Redskins had a play called "70 chip" they used in short-yardage situations. Such a situation presented itself late in the game when the Redskins faced fourth down and inches to go for a first

Riggins First Jet to 1,000 Yards

Fifteen seasons had passed for the Jets organization, and the team had never had a 1,000-yard rusher.

Enter the Diesel.

John Riggins joined the team in 1971 from the University of Kansas, and everybody knew he had special skills as a running back. He could run over a defender or run away from one, making him a rare breed.

Riggins rushed for 769 yards in his rookie season of 1971 and would likely have become the first Jets running back to surpass 1,000 yards in 1972 had he not missed the final two games of the season, finishing with 944 yards. He followed with 482 yards in 1973 and 680 in 1974 before reporting to the Jets in 1975 on a mission. Much of that mission dealt with him feeling he'd been slighted on his contract with the Jets. Riggins decided to play out his option in 1975, which would make him a free agent after the 1975 season.

Riggins had learned that the NFL was a business, and he understood that in order for him to realize the kind of contract he wanted once he left the Jets for greener pastures, he would have to produce on the field.

In the second week of the 1975 season, Riggins had his first 100-yard game of the season when he rushed 27 times for 145 yards in a 30–24 win against the Kansas City Chiefs. He did not have another 100-yard game until the seventh week of the season, when he rushed for 108 yards in a 24–23 loss to the Buffalo Bills. Seven games was the halfway point of a 14-game NFL season in 1975, and Riggins had accrued 451 yards to that point.

The Jets had a dismal team in 1975, which made passing the more prevalent option on offense, since the team always seemed to be trailing. That fact made Riggins' task even more taxing. For example, in a 52–19 loss against the Colts in Baltimore in the ninth week of the season, Riggins carried the ball just eight times for 14 yards.

Nevertheless, Riggins used a 152-yard rushing effort against the New England Patriots in the 12th week of the season to springboard him toward a 1,000-yard season. He gained 75 yards the following week against the San Diego Chargers before rushing

12 times for 62 yards in the Jets' final game of the season against the Dallas Cowboys.

Riggins finished with 1,005 yards for the season on 238 carries to become the first Jets running back to surpass 1,000 yards. Sadly for the Jets and their fans, that would be his final season with the team.

down. Quarterback Joe Theismann handed the ball to the Diesel, and he broke a tackle then went the distance for a 43-yard touchdown. The Redskins won the game 27–17, and Riggins won MVP honors for establishing a new Super Bowl rushing record of 166 yards on 38 carries.

"He's a character, but on the football field he was a special package, because he had the size, speed, and the hands," Joe Namath told the *New York Times*. "He could do everything. He could break away from cornerbacks. He could outrun people and had the power to hit up inside. He was inside and outside."

Riggins entered the Hall of Fame in 1992. At the induction ceremony in Canton, he was the last to speak, and commissioner Paul Tagliabue introduced him, to which the always outrageous Riggins had a funny retort.

"It is indeed a pleasure to be here, but we've been here too long," Riggins said. "Everybody wants to know why I asked the commissioner to introduce me. Well, Madonna had a headache."

He went on to tell the audience that if he had offended anybody over the years, he had not meant to do so.

"I tried to be honest," Riggins said. "I've been described as a man who walked to a beat of a different drummer, and I'm not sure that is right. If you had some of the things happen to you that I have, you might have reacted the same way. As I advise a lot of young athletes, aim high and shoot straight. That's what I tried to do."

John Riggins was one of a kind.

24 Sonny Werblin

New York's American Football League franchise had reached the bottom by 1962.

Nobody showed up to the games at the Polo Grounds, the team wasn't winning, and Harry Wismer, the team's owner, had financial difficulties. That's when the Gotham Football Club, headed by entertainment executive Sonny Werblin, entered the picture in February 1963 to buy the team from Wismer for $1 million, which essentially came down to Werblin and his partners assuming the team's debt.

Werblin and company got off to a rousing start with the team in 1963. They changed the team's colors from blue and gold to white and green and changed the team's name from Titans to Jets in advance of the team's moving from the Polo Grounds to Shea Stadium.

Additional momentum was gained for the "other" New York professional football franchise when they selected Ohio State's Matt Snell with the first selection of the 1964 draft. The Ohio State running back had also been selected by the New York Giants in the NFL Draft, but Werblin managed to sign him for the Jets, thereby bringing in one of the major building blocks for the team's future greatness.

Werblin was accustomed to success, which he had found throughout his professional career. After graduating from Rutgers University, he parlayed his degree into a job with Music Corporation of America, where he rose up the ladder to become president of the company's television division. He understood the media, which clearly gave him vision when the 1965 AFL Draft (which actually took place on November 28, 1964) rolled around and the Jets selected Joe Namath with the first overall pick of the draft.

The St. Louis Cardinals had also selected Namath in the NFL Draft, making him the 12th overall pick, so many assumed that the talented gunslinger would sign with the more established league. This is where Werblin stepped in on behalf of his team.

Werblin recognized Namath's star power and felt as though that would lead his team to the place it needed to go. So Werblin opened up his checkbook and enticed Namath to join the Jets after working out a deal with him worth $427,000.

Though the three-year deal included jobs for two of Namath's brothers in the total, the amount caught the attention of the American public, as no player had ever been issued such a deal when moving from the collegiate ranks to professional football. Making the amount of the contract known only served to make Namath more of a celebrity. Fans wanted to see the guy who was worth all this money—whether to succeed or fail—making Namath an instant star while suddenly making the Jets one of the most visible teams in sports.

"He knew the value of the fan and the star system," Namath told the *New York Times* upon Werblin's death in 1981. "Over the years, he adopted me. He made sure I was getting along well. He told me to get to know New York, that it was the greatest city."

Of course Namath proved to be more than a drawing card as he led the Jets to victory in Super Bowl III.

Sadly for Werblin, his popularity as the owner of the Jets led to his demise.

Werblin's partners grew jealous of his high visibility—even though he actually became a popular part of the Jets that drew fans to the product—so they bought him out for $1.2 million prior to the start of the 1968 season. Werblin made a nice profit, since his initial share of the team had cost him $250,000, but he was not with the team when Namath led them to their monumental Super Bowl victory in 1969.

Though no longer with the Jets, Werblin maintained a presence on the New York sports scene, running Madison Square Garden and later helping to create Meadowlands Sports Complex in New Jersey.

 **Matt Snell**

A successful passing team always has needed a complimentary running game in order to survive. The Jets' passing game of the late 1960s and early 1970s had just that, thanks in large part to Matt Snell, one of the team's first legitimate stars.

Snell graduated from Carle Place (New York) High School and headed to the Midwest to play his college ball at Ohio State, where he was a three-year starter at several positions. He played halfback in 1961, defensive end in 1962, and in his final year with the Buckeyes he moved to fullback, which made him the featured back.

Snell had been a standout defensive end, but he made the transition to fullback and excelled, winning team MVP honors while enticing the Jets to draft him in the first round of the 1964 AFL Draft and the New York Giants to select him in the fourth round of the NFL Draft.

Snell signed with the Jets and continued to excel in his rookie season in the AFL in 1964 by rushing for 945 yards en route to winning the AFL Rookie of the Year Award.

The 945 yards gained during his rookie season would be the high-water mark of his professional career due in large part to the presence of fellow running back Emerson Boozer, who combined with Snell to give the Jets an imposing tandem of running backs.

Snell is best remembered for his hard-nosed style of play and for his performance in Super Bowl III when many felt Snell—and not Joe Namath—should have won the MVP Award.

The Baltimore Colts were 18-point favorites for Super Bowl III and entered the game expecting a passing bonanza by Namath. Instead the Colts defense found out the hard way that the Jets had a hard-nosed running game.

Injuries began to mount for Snell, and he retired following the 1972 season after making three Pro Bowls and once earning All-Pro honors. In nine professional seasons, all with the Jets, Snell gained 4,285 yards, averaging 4.1 yards per carry and scoring 24 touchdowns.

Snell maintained a high profile after his retirement, appearing in the first Miller Lite beer commercial. The commercials featured retired sports stars and gained great popularity in the 1970s.

Rex Ryan

After the Jets fired Eric Mangini following the 2008 season, Rex Ryan became the 17th coach in team history on January 21, 2009.

Initially, most knew Ryan as the son of former NFL coach Buddy Ryan, who gained a high profile as the defensive coordinator for the Chicago Bears in the 1980s. Buddy Ryan was also the head coach for the Philadelphia Eagles and Arizona Cardinals. But Rex Ryan had more than paid his dues by the time the Jets brought him into the fold.

Rex Ryan throws the ball around at Jets minicamp at the New Meadowlands Stadium on June 16, 2010.

Rex played defensive end at Southwestern Oklahoma State, where his twin brother, Rob, also played football. Following his college days, Ryan coached at Eastern Kentucky, New Mexico Highlands, and Morehead State before joining his father in Arizona as the Cardinals' defensive-line/linebackers coach from 1994 to 1995. Ryan then moved back to the collegiate ranks, serving as the defensive coordinator at Cincinnati and Oklahoma before becoming the defensive-line coach for the Baltimore Ravens in 1999, where he became an integral part of the Super Bowl XXXV champion team.

Ryan worked as the Ravens' defensive-line coach for five years before moving up to assume the role as the team's defensive coordinator in 2005.

Prior to the 2008 season, Ravens head coach Brian Billick was fired along with the entire staff. Ryan, who had been voted the NFL's Assistant Coach of the Year by *Pro Football Weekly* and the Pro Football Writers Association in 2006, interviewed to become Billick's replacement, but the Ravens hired John Harbaugh. Ryan had a relationship with Harbaugh from their days coaching at the University of Cincinnati, and Harbaugh opted to keep him with the Ravens, promoting him to defensive coordinator/assistant head coach.

During Ryan's 10 seasons with the Ravens, the Ravens' defense never ranked lower than sixth in the NFL. The Ravens ranked first for fewest points allowed (17.1 per game), fewest rushing yards allowed per game (87.3), most shutouts (9), most takeaways (337), most interceptions (212), most interceptions for touchdowns (29), and third-down-conversion defense (33.9 percent).

So Ryan had more than earned his shot when the Jets decided to give him a chance.

Like his father, Ryan was not one to shy away from being controversial or outspoken. After the Jets gave Ryan a 24–7 win over the Texans at Houston in his first regular-season game as the Jets' coach, Ryan endeared himself to Jets fans with one of his comments on the radio the week leading up to their home opener against the New England Patriots in Week 2 of the season. Ryan boldly stated, "I didn't come here to kiss Bill Belichick's rings."

The Patriots, of course, had won three Super Bowls with Belichick calling the shots, but Ryan was not intimidated, and neither were his Jets, who defeated the Patriots 16–9. New Yorkers love a little swagger, especially if the person with that swagger can back it up. Ryan earned some instant street cred.

He further minted himself as a fan favorite when the Jets won their final two games of the season—beating the undefeated Indianapolis Colts in Indianapolis and the Cincinnati Bengals in the final sporting event held at Giants Stadium—to advance to the playoffs for the first time since the 2006 season.

The Jets won twice in the playoffs before bowing out 30–17 to the Colts in the AFC Championship Game.

Not only had the Jets found themselves a personality in Rex Ryan, they had also found themselves a football coach.

27 Giants Stadium

Giants Stadium, also known as the Meadowlands, became the new venue for Jets football games in 1984 after the team left its previous home, Shea Stadium.

Because Jets fans do not like to use the *G* word, we'll refer to Giants Stadium as the Meadowlands.

The New Jersey state legislature created the New Jersey Sports and Exposition Authority on May 10, 1971, with the purpose of financing, constructing, and administering a sports complex with a

Gate *D* Experience

Pro football halftime shows have traditionally brought an endless display of yawners. Even during the early days when more entertainment was provided, the composition of the acts would be something along the lines of Up with People or a dog chasing a Frisbee, leaving much to be desired.

Leave it to Jets fans to come up with their own form of entertainment, albeit a far cry from family entertainment.

Jets fans are not unlike other pro football fans in that they enjoy a cold beer or two, which leads to the requisite bathroom break at appropriate moments like halftime. A custom began to evolve sometime during the 2005 season when male Jets fans left the inside of Giants Stadium to use the facilities and perhaps enjoy a smoke at the intermission. While standing at a Gate *D* pedestrian ramp, men began to make catcalls and whistles to women to expose their breasts.

Occasionally a woman or two would comply, and the masses would howl with delight like a bachelor party at the local strip club. Finally, in November 2007, the *New York Times* reported on this behavior, and shortly thereafter beefed-up security ensured that said behavior was curtailed.

75,000-seat stadium for football and a racetrack. Through the powers granted through the legislature, the Authority could borrow money, issue bonds, lease property, and conduct horse racing. Financing for the project came from revenue bonds backed by state-run racetrack proceeds, which allowed the complex to be built and operated with no expense to the taxpayers.

Construction of the stadium and the racetrack began in 1972. In September 1976, the Meadowlands racetrack opened, and the football stadium opened on October 10, 1976, with its lone football tenant, the Giants, playing the Dallas Cowboys in front of a packed house.

On September 6, 1984, the Jets played their first game at the Meadowlands and came out on the losing end of a 23–17 affair with the Pittsburgh Steelers. The Jets would spend their next 24 seasons playing at the New Jersey venue.

When the Jets left for the Meadowlands, most figured the stadium would be renamed. After all, having the Jets play in Giants Stadium had a disturbing feel to all Jets fans. Alas, the Giants had to approve such a change and would not do so. So even though the Jets would begin playing all of their home games at the Meadowlands, the stadium would reflect the name of their longtime rival, while giving Jets fans more cause to dislike the Giants.

Helping to cope with the unfortunate matter of the stadium's name, a makeover occurred prior to every Jets game that would see Jets-green banners cover the walls and Jets logos covering the outside gates in an effort to hide any traces of the Giants' colors, red and blue.

Dual occupancy did make the Meadowlands unique, and after a Jets-Dolphins game on September 14, 2003, the stadium earned the distinction of having hosted the most NFL games in league history, surpassing Wrigley Field, where the Chicago Bears played for 50 years.

Another unique offshoot came with a mid-December tradition that would see the stadium host the Giants on Saturday and the Jets on Sunday, or vice versa, during a Saturday-Sunday NFL double-header, prompting considerable work for the stadium's grounds crew in preparing the field for the Sunday game.

In addition, the Jets play the Giants once every four years, thanks to NFL schedule-makers, which offers the opportunity for either the Jets or the Giants to play one of their road games at home.

According to legend, Jimmy Hoffa is buried under one of the end zones at the Meadowlands. Fueling that contention is the fact that the disappearance of the infamous labor leader came at approximately the same time the stadium was built.

The Jets earned the distinction of playing in the first NFL playoff game at the Meadowlands when they hosted an AFC Wild Card game against the Patriots on December 28, 1985; the Patriots won 26–14.

In the final game played at the Meadowlands on January 3, 2010, the Jets defeated the Cincinnati Bengals 37–0. Shortly after, the Meadowlands began to meet its demise on February 4, 2010, when the demolition of the stadium began, leaving behind many memories—and perhaps a corpse.

28 First Jets-Giants Regular-Season Contest

Sooner or later the inevitable had to happen and the Jets would get to meet the New York Giants in a regular-season game. Unfortunately for the Jets, their first meeting with the Giants came at a time when three of the team's best players were unavailable for duty.

The much-awaited first regular-season contest between New York's two professional football teams came on November 1, 1970, at Shea Stadium. Not playing for the Jets were quarterback Joe Namath, who was out with a wrist injury; fullback Matt Snell, who had a ruptured heel tendon; and running back Emerson Boozer, with torn rib cartilage.

In essence, these injuries stymied the Jets' running and passing games.

Meanwhile, the Giants were riding high on the wings of a three-game winning streak fueled by media darling Fran Tarkenton. The Jets' injuries and Tarkenton's prowess prompted oddsmakers to install the Giants as nine-point favorites.

Despite the Jets being dinged up, the contest still held special meaning for New Yorkers, who realized you could either be a Jets fan or a Giants fan, but you could not be both. Both factions understood that—until the two teams would meet again in 1974— bragging rights would belong to the team that won.

Due to the interest in the game, the blackout was lifted, and the game was shown on a local channel.

On the bright side for the Jets, standout receivers Don Maynard and George Sauer were healthy and ready to play, meaning the Jets had four quality receivers, including rookie stand-outs Eddie Bell and Rich Caster. But even if the receivers were open, could backup quarterback Al Woodall successfully connect with them?

Any pressure entering the game rested squarely on the shoulders of the Giants. Not only were New York bragging rights at stake, the Giants' playoff hopes were on the line as well. If they wanted to have a chance at winning the Eastern Division of the NFC, they could not lose.

Jets players embraced their underdog role, and once the game began, they played like a team with nothing to lose, taking a 10–3 lead and then holding the Giants one foot from scoring a touch-down with five minutes left in the third quarter.

Tarkenton got irate at a late tackle by Jets linebacker Larry Grantham on the play, which provoked a brief brawl between the two clubs. Once order was restored, the Jets had the momentum, but they were in a dangerous situation sitting 12 inches from their own goal line.

Woodall sought counsel from Jets coach Weeb Ewbank, who told him the best course of action would be to go with a quarter-back sneak in order to gain a little breathing room.

Woodall hit the line on the next two plays and gained nothing. Facing a third down, the Jets called Chuck Mercein's number. Mercein was a journeyman NFL running back who had played for the Giants and the Green Bay Packers and was signed two weeks earlier due to the decimated nature of the Jets' backfield.

Mercein took the handoff and was met in the end zone by Giants middle linebacker Jim File, thereby recording a safety for the Giants to cut the Jets' lead to 10–5.

Suddenly momentum swung in the Giants' direction.

As dictated by the safety, the Jets had to kick off from their own 20. The Giants received the football and got to work, with Tarkenton quickly throwing scoring strikes to Bob Tucker and Clifton McNeil to put the Giants up 19–10. The Jets' reversal of fortune had seen the Giants click on the two scoring passes within 77 seconds of each other.

The Giants added a field goal in the fourth quarter, and the first Jets-Giants regular-season game was history: Giants 21, Jets 10.

The Polo Grounds

The Polo Grounds had seen better days long before the New York Titans became a tenant of the historic ballpark in 1960.

The Titans played their home games at the Polo Grounds for the first four years of their existence—playing as the Jets in the last of those four years in 1963.

Originally the field was built in 1876 to facilitate the sport of polo. Three more fields were built that would hold the same name, but only the original hosted polo. The final rendition of the Polo Grounds became the most famous of the four.

Noteworthy for the final structure was the bathtub shape. For baseball this translated to a deep center field with short distances to the right- and left-field walls.

The New York baseball Giants were the original tenant of the Polo Grounds and continued to play at the facility through 1957. After that season, they moved to San Francisco. The Yankees sublet the Polo Grounds from the Giants with them from 1913 to 1922 before crossing the Hudson River to play at Yankee Stadium. Babe Ruth actually caught the baseball world's attention with some of the tape-measure home runs he hit at the Polo Grounds.

During the Giants' stay at the field, Willie Mays' over-the-shoulder catch of Vic Wertz's drive in the 1954 World Series and Bobby Thomson's famous home run in 1951 off Ralph also known as "the Shot Heard 'Round the World"—rank as the two most famous plays that took place in the stadium's lengthy history, though there were other memorable moments. Included in those were the 1923 heavyweight championship fight between Jack Dempsey and Luis Firpo and the 1941 fight where Joe Louis managed to dodge a colossal upset when he finished off Billy Conn with a late knockout.

The New York Football Giants played at the Polo Grounds before moving to Yankee Stadium in 1956. During their stay they hosted the 1934, 1938, 1944, and 1946 NFL Championship Games; they would move to Yankee Stadium in 1956.

Until the Titans moved in, the Polo Grounds had been without a tenant for three years. They were joined by the expansion New York Mets, who came into being in 1962 and played their first two seasons at the Polo Grounds until moving to brand-new Shea Stadium in Queens in 1964.

The Jets had the distinction of playing in the final sporting event at the Polo Grounds, where they lost 19–10 to the Buffalo Bills on December 14, 1963.

Eventually the city of New York managed to claim the land where the Polo Grounds sat under eminent domain. After success-fully doing so, they were able to condemn the stadium, which led to the demolition of the Polo Grounds in April 1968, a year before the Mets would win the World Series and the Jets would win the Super Bowl.

When the actual demolition took place, the wrecking ball that had been used on the demolition of Ebbets Field in 1964 was used to execute the same job on the Polo Grounds. The wrecking ball had been painted to resemble a baseball and managed to finish the job on its second historic ballpark after four months of work.

The Polo Grounds Towers public-housing project opened in 1968, erasing any evidence of where the historic ballpark had once stood and where the Jets had come into being.

30 Read *Semi-Tough*

Since the Jets and Giants have never met in a Super Bowl, any Jets fan should do the next-best thing, which is to dust off a fictional classic. We're not talking *Ulysses* here, rather a sports fictional classic by the humorous, cantankerous, and often politically incorrect Dan Jenkins.

Jenkins, a longtime sportswriter who often wrote for *Sports Illustrated*, penned *Semi-Tough* in 1972, and the book was later made into a movie starring Burt Reynolds, Kris Kristofferson, and Jill Clayburgh. But the movie did not capture the story or characters in the same flavor presented by Jenkins.

Yes, the book is crude, sometimes homophobic, and at times a little too graphic for the tastes of some, but make no mistake, this masterpiece will leave most readers laughing hysterically at the story that takes place primarily during the week before a Super Bowl confrontation between the Jets and Giants.

The only downside for Jets fans comes in the fact that the story's narrator, Billy Clyde Puckett, plays for the Giants.

Puckett is the Giants' star halfback and is writing a book while prepping to play the "dog-ass" Jets in the Super Bowl. Ironic is the fact that the crosstown rivals must fly across the country to meet in California for the big game. His closest friends are Giants wide receiver Shake Tiller, who also attended TCU with him, and Barbara Jane Bookman, who turns out to be his love interest.

Readers are privy to a lot of clever and down-to-earth dialogue straight from Puckett's native Texas as they experience life in the NFL during the week of the Super Bowl. Jets fans will wish the team had a player the caliber of Dreamer Tatum, a rover back for Jenkins' fictional Jets. Tatum's nickname comes from his days at USC when he hit so hard he often put opposing players to sleep. Puckett notes that all anybody ever sees while watching films of the Jets is Tatum "sticking some poor sumbitch in the gizzle when the poor sumbitch has tried to run a sweep."

Puckett notes that Shake and he would like to know Tatum better because they are fans of the way he plays, but, as Puckett explains, such a friendship would be hard to come by, not because Tatum plays for the "dog-ass" Jets, rather he lives on Long Island, where most of the Jets live, unlike the Giants players, who mostly live in Manhattan.

Along the way, Puckett and company head to several parties with the beautiful people who inhabit Super Bowl happenings. One such person they encounter amid the many sweeties and big shots is a Jets fan who doesn't mind telling Tiller what he believes his beloved Jets will do to the Giants. The encounter is priceless, and all Jets fans should remember that it's nice to be able to enjoy a laugh at one's own expense. So sit down and, in Jenkins' words, nurse a "young scotch" while you read and laugh along.

The actual game action during the Super Bowl brings into play some interesting scenarios and some vintage scenes involving T.J. Lambert, who is the Giants' somewhat exaggerated characterization of a defensive lineman.

I won't tell you which team wins the fictional encounter between the two New York football teams, but I will clue you in that Dreamer's performance would make any Jets fan proud. Though the movie was semienjoyable, the book is far different and much more entertaining.

Sports Illustrated's Top 100 Sports Books of All Time ranked *Semi-Tough* seventh.

31 Smith's 106-Yard Return

Most kickoff-return men understand one of the cold, hard facts of the job: you don't field a ball in your own end zone and try to make the return.

To do otherwise is to make your coach cringe, and making your coach cringe is one of the quickest tickets out of the NFL.

Said factoid did not keep Brad Smith from fielding a kickoff six yards deep in his end zone against the Indianapolis Colts on December 27, 2009. The rest of the story brought magic.

Smith played quarterback at the University of Missouri, where he was a four-year starter for the Tigers and attracted enough attention after his senior year that the Jets drafted him in the fourth round of the 2006 NFL Draft and projected him as a multipurpose player who could be used at quarterback, running back, wide receiver, and on special teams.

Smith became an integral weapon for the Jets in 2009 when head coach Rex Ryan used him in his Wildcat and Seminole formations, which featured him lining up at quarterback and running, much as he did while at Missouri.

In the 15th game of the 2009 season, the Jets traveled to Indianapolis to play the undefeated Colts. While the Colts were a lock for the playoffs, the Jets needed a win to remain in contention.

Smith already had received two kickoffs and downed them in the end zone by the time he caught the kickoff to start the second half with the Jets trailing 9–3. Looking to make something happen, special-teams coordinator Mike Westhoff had given Smith the go-ahead to return a kick out of the end zone if he found one to his liking and thought he could make a play. Indianapolis kicker Pat McAfee got his toe into the football, prompting Smith to backpedal into the end zone. At that point Westhoff gasped, watching Smith's next move, and quickly regretted giving him the green light upon seeing Smith exercise his option from six yards deep in the end zone.

The strategy on the play called for Smith to try and reach the blocking wedge in front of him as soon as possible. Smith managed to quickly reach the wedge, then followed his blockers while breaking to the outside en route to the sideline. Smith received excellent blocks on the play from Rob Turner, James Ihedigbo, Eric Smith, and Wallace Wright. Suddenly the playing field opened up with Smith needing to pass just one final obstacle in the form of Tim Jennings, the last Colts player Smith needed to get past to go all the way. When Jennings dove in vain, it became clear that Smith would score, thereby setting off a celebration on the Jets' sideline.

Ryan confessed after the game that he wasn't initially happy that Smith opted to return the kick.

"I'm like, 'Well, stay in and take a knee,'" Ryan told *Newsday*. "Then I'm like, 'Uh-oh' and then, 'Great job.' We felt good about our return chances, and Brad did a great job. He had super blocking. It really lifted us."

The Colts removed most of their starters in the second half, and the Jets went on to take a 29–15 win.

"When it happened, it didn't really feel like a big momentum-changer," Smith told *Newsday*. "I just felt like I was doing my job. That's what Westhoff always tells us. But looking back on it, I think it was a game-changer."

Smith's return stands as the longest play in Jets history, surpassing Aaron Glenn's 104-yard touchdown return of a missed field goal.

32 Attend Jets Training Camp

While training camp can be pure misery to the players, it's pure delight for the fans.

Any true Jets fan needs to attend training camp to gain a better understanding of the team. Camp begins in late July and, while there is plenty to see during camp, don't count on being able to see your favorite player on any given day due to the mysterious maladies that always seem to appear once the sun gets its hottest and the grind of training camp begins to weigh on the players.

Most practices are open to the public and offer the first chance to see the latest acquisitions and draft choices prior to the start of the regular season. Like at spring-training contests for baseball, training camp affords fans an opportunity to see the players close enough to mingle with a player or two while also scoring a coveted autograph.

Any training camp always brings questions about the team.

Is a certain player healthy for the coming season? Will the new quarterback be able to run the offense? Who will take the place of the standout player who retired? All are good questions that can be speculated upon during any off-season, and the answers to the questions can be seen through your own eyes during a workout.

Training camp is different things to different players.

For rookies and undrafted players, camp is all about trying to win a spot on the team. The zeal displayed by some players in this situation can often make attending a practice worthwhile. Making an impression usually comes with a big hit, always being the first one to the football, or a breakaway run.

At the other end of the spectrum are the guys like quarterback Mark Sanchez, who is at camp to fine-tune the offense, work with some new players to get their timing down, and perhaps add some different offensive packages to what they already run. Sanchez and other players like him don't have to worry about making the team, but they have to be on their toes to play hard in order to avoid any kind of injury that might delay or end their seasons.

During the first two or three days of camp, the practices are more of a lighter variety, with the players in a helmet and shorts. By the fourth or fifth day of practice, the players are wearing full pads. If there is a must-see day, the first day players are in pads would be the pick. Players have not hit anybody since the previous season, so nerves are frayed, and there's some added excitement. Usually the coaches are pushing the players a little extra on that first day in full pads just to get an idea about the physical character of each individual player—particularly the ones they have not seen before.

Focusing on someone like Sanchez—is he making the right reads, does he appear to have command of the team, are his passes crisp?—is certainly something of great interest to watch. For the more astute football fan, observing the harmony of the line play will likely be a more accurate litmus test for what the team will be like for the coming season. If the Jets have a quality offensive line, you can bet their season is going to be far more successful than if they are constantly trying to fill gaps on their front.

And there's always a new running back or receiver in camp who's likely to catch your eye and make you pull for him to make the team.

All the while, there's a chance of witnessing some great theater when a player hasn't done his homework and gets caught in the wrong spot on defense or runs a play differently than what was called on offense. Coaches have been known to blow a player's hair back on said occasions.

Currently the Jets hold training camp in Cortland, New York, at SUNY Cortland Stadium Complex. For more up-to-date details go to www.newyorkjets.com.

33 Mark Sanchez

Mark Sanchez became the Jets' first pick in the 2009 NFL Draft and the fifth player taken overall, which provided quite an eye-opener since even the overly cynical Jets fans could not boo the selection of the quarterback from the University of Southern California.

During Sanchez's junior season at Southern Cal in 2008, he led the Trojans to a 12–1 record, culminating with a win in the Rose Bowl that saw Sanchez win MVP honors. Following the season, he opted to leave school. Having red-shirted one year, Sanchez managed to graduate with a degree in communications.

Also speaking to Sanchez's character was the example he set for the Mexican-American population while at USC; he is a third-generation Mexican-American. Given the fact that USC is located in Los Angeles, which is home to approximately 3 million Mexicans, Sanchez became hugely popular. Grasping the extent of

Mark Sanchez prepares to pass during the AFC Championship Game in Indianapolis on January 24, 2010.

his popularity, Sanchez, who spoke some Spanish but was hardly bilingual, began to take Spanish lessons so he did not have to use a translator when doing interviews with the Spanish-speaking media.

The Jets signed Sanchez to a five-year deal worth $50 million, including $28 million in guarantees, which was the largest contract in team history. Jets fans sensed a Namath-like charisma in the handsome Sanchez that made him an instant favorite. Would the team finally have the quarterback they had long desired to take them to the promised land?

Heading into training camp, Sanchez ranked second on the quarterback depth chart. By the end of August, Sanchez had won the starting job, putting him behind center for the Jets in their season opener in Houston against the Texans on September 13, 2009.

The rookie quarterback drew rave reviews for throwing for a touchdown and 272 yards in a 24–7 Jets win. He followed his sizzling debut by leading the Jets to a 16–9 win over the New England Patriots at the Meadowlands, giving the Jets their first victory over the Patriots at home since the 2000 season. Suddenly New York had a new and exciting star.

Sanchez on Broadway

After one season with the Jets, Mark Sanchez had heard more than enough comparisons to Joe Namath, the Jets Hall of Fame quarterback.

Of course, Namath was "Broadway Joe" while it seems Sanchez is simply a fan of Broadway.

Upon taking up residence in New York City, Sanchez fell in love with the theater after seeing the Broadway production of *Wicked*.

Particularly enthralling to Sanchez was the fact that the actors experienced much of what he experienced during football games by having to live in the moment. Live productions do not allow for doing a scene until they get it right like they do in the movies, meaning stage actors had to nail it or fail in their roles.

Count *Billy Elliot*, *In the Heights*, and *Memphis* among Sanchez's favorite productions, and whenever possible, Sanchez likes to go behind the stage after a show to meet the actors. If you happen to see Sanchez passing you in traffic, there's a good chance you might catch him singing the lyrics to the soundtrack of one of his favorite productions.

Sanchez experienced a true thrill for any theater lover at the 64th annual Tony Awards when he was invited to be a presenter for the show that took place at Radio City Music Hall approximately a month before the beginning of training camp for his second season in the NFL.

Sanchez introduced a number from the musical *Memphis*, and he looked suave and composed when he told the audience, "I've become a huge fan of musicals since I've come to New York, and I've taken some heat from guys on the team, believe me."

The Jets' quarterback has pledged to try and induce some of his teammates to join him at future plays.

Sanchez suffered a sprained PCL in the game against the Buffalo Bills the first week of December, which caused him to miss the team's next game and brought concerns about whether the Jets could make the playoffs if Sanchez did not make a full recovery. He eased some of those concerns with his performance against undefeated Indianapolis in the Jets' 15th game of the season, proving to be a cool customer in a 29–15 win that handed the Colts their first loss while keeping alive the Jets' playoff hopes.

With Sanchez running the offense, the Jets beat the Cincinnati Bengals 37–0 in their final game of the season. In doing so, they earned a spot in the playoffs for the first time since the 2006 season.

In the Jets' first playoff game against the Bengals, Sanchez led the team to a 24–14 win in Cincinnati that saw the rookie complete 12 of 15 passes for 182 yards and a touchdown.

By leading his team to victory, Sanchez became the fourth rookie quarterback in NFL history to win his first playoff game.

The following week, Sanchez and company took a 17–14 win over the San Diego Chargers to lead his team into the AFC Championship Game, where Sanchez's glorious first season finally came to a close in a 30–17 loss to the Colts in Indianapolis.

The *Sporting News* named Sanchez to their All-Rookie team. Great things are expected in the years to come from the Jets' charismatic quarterback.

34 Shea Stadium

Shea Stadium may as well have been Camelot for Jets fans, given the era that ushered in the team's transition to the new venue that would play host to its games.

After spending the first four years of the team's existence at the dilapidated Polo Grounds—first as the Titans, then as the Jets—the Jets became tenants of Shea Stadium in 1964.

In addition to serving as the new home of the Jets, the new multipurpose stadium would also play host to the National League's expansion entry, the New York Mets. Flushing Meadow Park Municipal Stadium was to be the original name of the park located within a whisper of LaGuardia Airport. In the end, the park bore the name of William A. Shea, a New York lawyer generally credited with bringing National League baseball back to New York after the Dodgers and Giants had headed to California.

The construction of Shea Stadium cost $28.5 million and took 29 months to complete, bringing to life New York's grand new sports palace on April 17, 1964, with a 4–3 Mets loss to the Pittsburgh Pirates.

The Jets called Shea Stadium home from 1964 to 1983. Joe Namath played his entire career at Shea Stadium, and the Jets became Super Bowl champions during their tenure at the Queens locale.

When Shea was set up for football, the field went from home plate toward the outfield on the natural surface.

Among the memorable Jets moments at Shea were three playoff games, which included a 27–23 win over the Oakland Raiders in the American Football League Championship Game, a 13–6 loss to the Kansas City Chiefs in a 1969 AFL Divisional Playoff Game, and a 31–27 loss to the Buffalo Bills in a 1981 AFC Wild Card Playoff Game.

Also of historical significance was the Jets' game against the Bills in 1973 when O.J. Simpson became the first player in NFL history to surpass 2,000 rushing yards in a single season.

Like many football tenants at multipurpose stadiums, the Jets ranked second behind the Mets in the pecking order at Shea. Scheduling problems presented the biggest challenge for the Jets, who were at the mercy of the Mets' schedule. During the 1970s, the Jets also battled maintenance problems. Eventually this led to the Jets moving to the Meadowlands after the 1984 season, where the facility catered more to the Jets while also adding 15,000 to the seating capacity.

On December 10, 1983, the Jets played their final game at Shea Stadium and came out on the losing end of a 34–7 rout by the Pittsburgh Steelers. After the game, fans pillaged the stadium while the scoreboard spoke of the future as it read, *N.J. Jets.*

In addition to the Jets moments created at Shea, there were plenty of Major League Baseball moments created by the Mets, who brought postseason baseball to the stadium in 1969, 1973, 1986, 1988, 1999, 2000, and 2006. The last game played at Shea Stadium took place on September 28, 2008, and saw the Mets lose to the Florida Marlins.

Of the other events that took place at Shea, none could trump the Beatles, who opened their 1965 North American tour there on August 15, 1965, with a crowd of 55,600 watching.

The demolition of the ballpark began on October 14, 2008. Today the site where Shea Stadium once sat is a parking lot for the new home of the Mets, Citi Field, where fans can find Shea's home plate, pitcher's mound, and bases featured.

35 The One That Got Away

Despite having to endure the drama and obstacles created by winning the Super Bowl, the Jets managed to finish first in the American Football League's Eastern Division in 1969.

The Jets had ranked third in passing offense and third in rushing offense en route to a 10–4 mark for the season that bested the Houston Oilers, who finished second in the division with a 6–6–2 record.

Due to the playoff system in place at the time, the Jets were scheduled to meet the Kansas City Chiefs in the first round. The Chiefs had finished second in the AFL Western Division with an 11–3 mark behind the Oakland Raiders, who went 13–1. Conversely, the Raiders would play the Oilers.

Joe Namath completed another banner season in 1969, completing 185 of 361 passes for 19 touchdowns, earning the Associated Press honors as Player of the Year.

After losing two of their first three games, the Jets went 9–2 in their final 11 games. So everything seemed to be falling into place for the team to make a run at repeating as AFL champions and returning to the Super Bowl.

Like most professional football teams at the end of a season, the Jets were a banged-up bunch heading into their December 10, 1969, meeting with the Chiefs.

Standout flanker Don Maynard had suffered a broken bone in his foot during a November 23 game against the Cincinnati Bengals, but he was optimistic he would be available for the game. Even having missed three games, Maynard ranked third in the AFL with 938 receiving yards. Then there was the concern of every Jets fan during this particular era: Namath's health.

In October 1969, Namath, at the age of 26, had predicted that the 1969 season would be his last in professional football due to the bad knees that had ailed him since his senior season at the University of Alabama in 1964.

"I don't even talk about my knees anymore," Namath told the *New York Times.* "They always hurt, and I guess they always will."

Namath did not dispute reports that if the Jets lost to the Chiefs, the game might be his finale, though he did offer to the

Times, "I'm not going to announce anything right now. I'll have to see how my knees feel next summer before training camp."

Braving chilling winds, a crowd of 62,977 showed up at Shea Stadium to see if the Jets could continue their march to another world championship.

The outcome of the game came down to a play that took place midway through the fourth quarter with the Chiefs leading 6–3. Virtually every Jets fans would relive the play over and over throughout the coming off-season. Having reached Kansas City's goal line on a pass-interference call, the Jets had unsuccessfully moved the ball on their first two cracks at pay dirt and now faced third down. Rather than pound the ball up the middle against the tough Chiefs front wall, Namath rolled to his right, looking toward Matt Snell. The Jets' fullback had tried to sneak out of the backfield unnoticed, but he had not fooled Jim Kearney and Bobby Bell, who were right with him. Namath could not throw into double coverage, so he zipped the ball into the turf.

The Jets had to settle for a Jim Turner field goal that tied the game.

After the field goal, Chiefs quarterback Len Dawson quickly moved his team up the field, finding Otis Taylor on a crossing pattern for a 61-yard gain before connecting with Gloster Richardson on a 19-yard touchdown to put the Chiefs up 13–6.

The Jets had four more possessions in the game, reaching the Chiefs' 16 then the 13 without being able to punch the ball into the end zone. Namath's final pass of the game went to Bake Turner— who played most of the game in place of Maynard—and was intercepted by Jim Marsalis in the end zone.

There would be no return trip to the Super Bowl.

The Chiefs took a 13–6 win and went on to defeat the Raiders in the AFL Championship Game before beating the Minnesota Vikings in Super Bowl IV.

36 The Last Jets Game at Shea Stadium

A lot of magical moments occurred for the Jets at Shea Stadium, and the team hoped one final piece of magic would take place in the team's last game at Shea—and in New York.

The Jets had a 7–7 record on December 10, 1983, heading into a Saturday afternoon contest with the Pittsburgh Steelers that marked the team's finale in New York after 24 seasons. After the 1983 season, the Jets would move to the Meadowlands in East Rutherford, New Jersey, where they would play all of their home games. Of more importance than the nostalgia of the day was the fact the Jets still had a chance to make the playoffs if they beat the Steelers then won on the road in their final game of the season.

The Steelers team the Jets faced that day had once been a great championship team that had grown long in the tooth after winning four Super Bowls in six seasons during its prime. Several of the players from those halcyon days still played for the team, including quarterback Terry Bradshaw and running back Franco Harris, who would both start against the Jets.

Not long after the opening kickoff, it became apparent that the Jets were not going to be in the playoffs, given the bite of the Steelers that day.

Bradshaw threw a 17-yard touchdown to Greg Garrity in the first quarter to put the Steelers up 7–0. In the second quarter, Bradshaw again went to the air to find Calvin Sweeney for a 10-yard touchdown, and Gary Anderson kicked field goals of 29 and 40 yards to put the Steelers up 20–0 at the half.

Bradshaw, who was making his first appearance since having elbow surgery 11 months earlier, had to leave the game after hurting his right arm. Ultimately, the finale at Shea Stadium turned out to be the finale for Pittsburgh's Hall of Fame quarterback as well, as he never played in another game. Meanwhile, Harris ground out his 47th 100-plus-yard game of his Hall of Fame career by rushing for 103 yards on 26 carries.

Pittsburgh hardly missed Bradshaw as Cliff Stoudt continued what Bradshaw had started in the first half. The heir apparent to Bradshaw hit Bennie Cunningham for a 13-yard touchdown in the third quarter and hooked up with Sweeney from 18 yards out in the fourth quarter.

Lam Jones got the Jets on the board in the third quarter, hauling in a 27-yard touchdown from Pat Ryan, but the score served as a mere blemish on the Steelers' line that December day.

Once the game got out of hand, the natives began to get restless. Yes, these were the same Jets who had once brought a Super Bowl to the city of New York. But now they were the losing franchise that was bolting from New York for greener pastures in New Jersey.

By the time the 34–7 Steelers rout concluded, a line of New York City's finest lined up underneath one goal post. Nevertheless, rowdy Jets fans stormed the field and managed to tear down both goal posts while running roughshod over Shea Stadium's turf. Along the way, many grabbed hunks of turf. Some of the hunks were carried away as keepsakes from 20 years of memories, while others were hurled at police officers, who sought shelter from the crowd by retreating to the home-plate end of the stadium, where protective glass offered them safety.

The Jets had one remaining game on their 1983 schedule, but essentially their season was over, given the fact that their playoff hopes had been dashed. They went on the road for their final game and lost 34–14 to the Dolphins to give them a 7–9 mark for the 1983 season. And Shea Stadium became a distant memory for the Jets.

37 Shake Fireman Ed's Hand

Ed Anzalone defines what it means to be a Jets fan.

Known as "Fireman Ed" due to the fact he is a New York City firefighter, Anzalone has been a recognizable figure sitting in Section 134 at the Meadowlands during Jets games since 1986. Everybody knew him as the guy wearing a Jets jersey and a fireman's helmet decorated like the home team's helmet—hoisted on the shoulders of his brother Frank—while leading the team's rallying cry from the stands: "J-E-T-S, Jets! Jets! Jets!" There is some debate as to whether he actually came up with the chant, but there can be no dispute that he knows how to lead it.

While every true Jets fan knows who Fireman Ed is, so do players from the opposing teams. Jason Taylor became the first to acknowledge Fireman Ed's existence.

When Taylor played for the Miami Dolphins, Fireman Ed reported being the target of Taylor's profanity after the Dolphins defeated the Jets at the Meadowlands. Taylor also mentioned Fireman Ed on a later date when outlining the extent of his disdain for Jets fans in general.

During one radio interview with Taylor, he characterized Giants fans as having more class than Jets fans, summing up his remarks by noting, "Jets fans take the *CL* out of *class*."

When asked by the *Daily News* to respond to Taylor's remarks, Fireman Ed said, "Jets fans have enthusiasm. We're not the wine-and-cheese, playing-at-1:00 fans. That's Giants fans. Jets fans are down and dirty. Let's get it done."

The 2009 season proved to be memorable for Fireman Ed, whom the Jets honored as the spokesman for all Jets fans with a

Fireman Ed sits on another fan's shoulders at a Jets-Patriots game at Giants Stadium on September 14, 2008.

game ball on September 25 after the Jets defeated the New England Patriots in their home opener.

The presentation of the game ball from Jets head coach Rex Ryan came at the Atlantic Health Jets Training Center in the second-floor dining area. Fireman Ed had two points he wanted to get across before stepping up for Jets fans everywhere to accept the presentation from head coach Rex Ryan in front of the team.

Fireman Ed spoke from the heart after receiving the ball, noting how much all of his fellow Jets fans would like to be where he stood and how they were just as worthy. He said, "Their passion is as great as mine is. There's no difference. I'm just blessed to be able to lead the orchestra, to get them crazy."

Fireman Ed pointed out that the crowd noise during the Jets' 16–9 win over the Patriots had been the loudest in memory. He then thanked Ryan and the team while declaring his allegiance as well as that of his fellow fans. At the conclusion of Fireman Ed's comments, Ryan offered a one-thumb-up salute to Jets fans and their leader, noting, "Thanks, fans."

Prior to the Jets' dismantling of the Cincinnati Bengals in the final week of the 2009 season, Fireman Ed again received recognition, this time from loquacious Bengals wide receiver Chad Ochocinco, who had made an art of post-touchdown theatrics. Ochocinco revealed that he planned to imitate Fireman Ed if he scored a touchdown, but Ochocinco did not catch a pass in the Bengals' 37–0 loss to the Jets.

Ochocinco offered Fireman Ed an olive branch for all of the lip service he had directed his way by getting in touch with him and inviting him to the Jets' first-round playoff game against the Bengals in Cincinnati. Though appreciative of the offer, Fireman Ed would not sell out and respectfully declined on the basis that he could not accept such a gesture from the opposing team.

Fireman Ed was enshrined in the Pro Football Hall of Fame in 1999 in the Hall of Fans section. Next time you're at a Jets game and you see Fireman Ed, go up to him and shake his hand.

38 Bill Parcells

Bill Parcells, also known as "the Big Tuna," joined the Jets in 1997, becoming the biggest fish to coach the team since Weeb Ewbank came over from the Baltimore Colts prior to the 1963 season.

Jets fans were more than familiar with the famed coach from his days as the coach of the New York Giants from 1983 through 1990.

The Giants won two Super Bowls under Parcells, first with a win over the Denver Broncos in Super Bowl XXI followed by a win over the Buffalo Bills in Super Bowl XXV. After coaching the Giants, Parcells went to New England and led the Patriots to a Super Bowl appearance against the Green Bay Packers, who defeated the Patriots in Super Bowl XXXI.

Jets fans were hopeful Parcells would use his coaching magic to lead their team to the place they had not reached since Ewbank had done so with Joe Namath at the helm in Super Bowl III.

Parcells went to the Jets following his retirement from football after coaching the New England Patriots. Even though he had retired, Parcells remained contractually obligated to the Patriots, meaning he could not coach another team. But when the Jets' interest became serious, a deal came to fruition that released Parcells from his contract. In return, the Patriots received a first-round draft choice, which seemed a fair deal if Parcells could get anywhere near the results he'd gotten in his other stops and could resurrect the team's fortunes after Rich Kotite's 4–28 tenure.

A change in attitude could be seen almost immediately, and that attitude change was reflected on the field as well.

Parcells knew how to motivate players, he understood the *X*s and *O*s of the game, and he didn't mind being the bad guy in order to get the job done. The Jets responded to their new coach in his

Medium-Difficulty Jets Trivia

These trivia questions aren't the hardest, but you might need to peruse the pages of this book a little bit in order to know the answers.

1. Which quarterback did the Jets draft from Marshall University in the 2000 NFL Draft and release prior to the 2008 season to make room for Brett Favre?
2. Who was the first coach in the history of the New York Jets franchise? (Hint: He was the first coach of the New York Titans.)
3. What historic New York stadium did the New York Titans call home during the inaugural season of the American Football League?
4. What team did Weeb Ewbank coach to the NFL championship in 1958?
5. Who scored the Jets' only touchdown in Super Bowl III?
6. Who is Rex Ryan's father?
7. What quarterback did the Miami Dolphins draft in the 1983 NFL Draft after the Jets selected quarterback Ken O'Brien?
8. Who set the NFL record for the longest punt while punting for the Jets?
9. Did Joe Namath lead another NFL team to a Super Bowl?
10. Where did Freeman McNeil attend college?

Answers:

1. Chad Pennington	5. Matt Snell	9. No
2. Sammy Baugh	6. Buddy Ryan	10. UCLA
3. The Polo Grounds	7. Dan Marino	
4. Baltimore Colts	8. Steve O'Neal	

first year on the job in 1997 when they went 9–7 after going 1–15 the previous season, which fueled high expectations for the 1998 season. To the delight of the white and green faithful, Parcells' Jets met those expectations head on, earning a spot in the playoffs in 1998 with a 12–4 record. After winning in the divisional playoffs, they lost to the Denver Broncos in the AFC Championship Game.

Once again the sky appeared to be the limit for the Jets in 1999. Unfortunately for Parcells and the team, quarterback Vinny

Testaverde suffered a ruptured Achilles tendon in the home opener, leading to a 1–6 start; the team never recovered. Though the team fought to finish at 8–8, Parcells opted to retire for the second time at the end of the season, having posted a 29–19 record during his three seasons coaching the Jets.

Parcells cited the fact that he no longer felt he could put forth the 365-days-a-year effort that coaching an NFL team required. In announcing his decision to retire, Parcells said, "I'm not going to coach anymore. This is definitely the end of my career."

In the weeks that followed Parcells' announcement, Al Groh was named to be his successor as the Jets' head coach.

Following his familiar pattern, Parcells returned to coaching with the Dallas Cowboys in 2003 and remained the team's head coach until retiring a third time in 2007, before eventually ending up in a management position with the Miami Dolphins.

Parcells' record as an NFL head coach is 172–130, which should be the final ledger for one of the league's all-time greatest coaches, but where Parcells is concerned, one never knows if he will make another return to the sideline.

39 Richard Todd

Could the Jets mine for gold in the same place and once again come away rich? That's what the Jets were trying to make happen when they returned to the University of Alabama to draft a quarterback with their first-round pick of the 1976 NFL Draft.

Richard Todd had many physical gifts, which he displayed while running Alabama's wishbone offense under the watchful eye of legendary coach Paul "Bear" Bryant.

While at Alabama, Todd never quarterbacked a losing game in the always-tough Southeastern Conference.

Todd stood 6'2" and weighed 210 pounds, had a strong arm, and could run the football, which he proved while running the wishbone. That in itself brought an interesting aspect to the decision regarding whether to draft Todd or not. Could he adapt to running a pro-style offense after running the college offense? Todd fueled the fire by winning Most Valuable Player honors in the Senior Bowl. Employing a pro-style offense, He passed for two touchdowns and 332 yards.

The Jets saw enough and selected him with the sixth overall pick that they had earned after finishing with a 3–11 record in 1975, which only added to the hype that Todd would become the savior to take over the Jets from Joe Namath. And why shouldn't Todd be the guy to do so? After all, Namath had played quarterback at Alabama, too.

The changing of the guard took place after the 1976 season, when the Jets released Namath and handed over the offense to the 23-year-old Todd. His learning curve proved to be long and painful for Jets fans. After five seasons with the Jets, he had thrown fewer touchdowns than interceptions. He did set an NFL record with 42 completions in 1980 during a loss to the Jets (later broken by Drew Bledsoe). But every Jets fan knew the record was tainted. The 49ers were winning big, prompting them to play a prevent zone defense. Pass after pass, Todd threw underneath the zone, connecting on the pass and gaining little as the time ran out in a 37–27 49ers win. More infamy came for Todd that same season as he threw 30 interceptions and set an NFL record by throwing at least one interception in 15 different games.

Todd finally came to life in 1981 and led the Jets to their first winning season since 1969, and with a record of 10–5–1 they earned a spot in the playoffs, but they lost in the AFC Wild Card Playoffs. His teammates selected him the team's Most Valuable

Player after a season that saw him set club records for passing attempts with 497 and completions with 279 while cutting down his interception total to 13.

Building on his success, Todd again led the Jets to the playoffs in 1982, guiding the team to victories over the Cincinnati Bengals and Los Angeles Raiders to earn a spot in the AFC Championship Game against the Miami Dolphins.

Todd could do little against the Dolphins as he struggled in a mud-covered field. At the end of the day, the Jets quarterback had thrown five interceptions and the Dolphins had a 14–0 win under their belt as they headed to the Super Bowl.

Todd's last season with the Jets came in 1983 when the Jets suffered through a 7–9 season. After the season, the Jets traded him to New Orleans, where he would play two more seasons before retiring after the 1985 season.

On the surface, Todd's career numbers look good, having completed 1,610 of his 2,967 passes for 124 touchdowns. But he also threw 161 interceptions and never truly reached the elite status forecast for him when he came out of college.

Pat Leahy

Pat Leahy arrived on the Jets in 1974 after attending St. Louis University, where he played on a soccer team that brought three NCAA national championships to the Billiken from 1969 to 1972.

The fact that Leahy played only soccer at St. Louis did not keep him from looking toward a more lucrative future in the NFL. In the shadow of Leahy's college, the NFL's St. Louis Cardinals held a tryout camp in 1974, and he got up the courage to attend—as did 200 other hopefuls. But when the tryout camp concluded, Leahy was the last man standing, which earned him an invitation to the Cardinals training camp in 1974. Unfortunately for Leahy, veteran Jim Bakken managed to retain his job, which turned into good fortune for the Jets.

Bobby Howfield had kicked for the Jets since 1971. When he got hurt, the door of opportunity flew open for Leahy. He played in six games in 1974, converting on six of 11 field-goal attempts. That season would lead to Leahy becoming the Jets' place kicker for what seemed like an eternity to most Jets fans.

All told, Leahy served as the Jets' kicker from 1974 through 1991, playing for five head coaches along the way while setting team records for games played with 250 and points with 1,470. Of the 426 field goals he attempted in his career—all with the Jets— Leahy made 304, which translated to 71.1 percent, and he converted 95.5 percent of his extra-point attempt. In addition, he kicked a 55-yard field goal, the longest in team history.

Leahy maintained that for a kicker to kick the ball straight, he needed to have his head straight. And he wasn't talking about posture, as he explained to *Boys' Life* in November 1991. "You try not to have any highs or lows," said Leahy, noting that if you let down your teammates, "you have to put it behind you."

Field-goal kickers don't hang around long if they aren't consistent. Leahy provided a model of consistency for the Jets. In 1986 he set a franchise record by connecting on 22 consecutive field-goal attempts. Jay Feely tied that record in 2009.

And, as much a tribute to Leahy as the Jets' special-teams unit, throughout his 18-year career Leahy never experienced the agony of having a kick blocked.

"The highlight, for me, was being able to stay and play in such a spotlighted market," Leahy told the *Daily News*. "There were

Brien's Miss

Doug Brien proved to be a reliable kicker during his two years with the Jets. Sadly for the veteran kicker from the University of California, Jets fans remember him for the one he didn't make.

Brien made 27 of 32 kicks for the Jets in 2003, good for 84.4 percent, and he made all 24 extra points he attempted. In 2004 he showed more of the same, kicking 24 field goals in 29 attempts, and he missed just one extra point in 34 attempts.

The Jets went 10–6 during the 2004 season under head coach Herman Edwards, which earned the team a spot in the playoffs. After defeating the San Diego Chargers 20–17 in the first wild-card round of the playoffs—when Brien kicked a 28-yard field goal to win the game in overtime—the Jets went to Pittsburgh to play the Steelers in the divisional round, which turned out to be a battle to see which team could earn a spot in the AFC Championship Game.

The Jets trailed early in the game when the Steelers surged to a 10–0 lead. Brien kicked a 42-yard field goal in the second quarter to make the score 10–3, then Santana Moss returned a punt 75 yards to tie the score at 10 at the half.

Momentum swung further in the Jets' direction when Reggie Tongue picked off a pass from Ben Roethlisberger and went 86 yards the other direction for a touchdown and a 17–10 third-quarter lead.

Roethlisberger took the Steelers in for a touchdown in the fourth quarter, culminating in a four-yard touchdown pass to Hines Ward that tied the score at 17.

With 2:02 left in regulation, Brien lined himself up for a 47-yard field goal to win the game. Instead, his kick hit the crossbar and bounded away. Brien had no time to sulk, because Jets cornerback David Barrett intercepted a Roethlisberger pass on the first play that the Steelers had the ball.

Brien would get another chance. This time he lined up from 43 yards out with six seconds remaining in regulation. But the ball went wide left, and the game went to overtime, where Pittsburgh's Jeff Reed connected from 33 yards out to give the Steelers a 20–17 win.

Afterward, Brien expressed his feelings about letting down the team.

"I feel bad for the team, for all the guys who played so well," Brien said. "This is going to take a while to get over."

Doug Brien's fate became the talk of the Gang Green faithful following that game. Realizing that Jets fans would likely never forgive Brien, the Jets did not bring him back the following season and replaced him with Mike Nugent.

some ups and downs, but I was able to stay for a long time. Being a college soccer player, I never even dreamed I'd get a tryout."

Leahy retired after the 1991 season at the age of 40, a year after he had been voted the team's Most Valuable Player. He made 26 of 37 attempts during the 1991 season as well as all of his extra-point attempts, so performance did not force him to retire, as a bad back did the trick.

A lot of players came and went during Leahy's tenure as the Jets' place kicker. Joe Namath was the team's quarterback when he arrived, and Browning Nagle held that distinction when he retired. Jets fans fondly remember Leahy as the best special-teams player in club history.

41 Keyshawn Johnson

The Jets held the coveted first selection of the NFL Draft in 1996.

A lot of talented players were available that year—such as Jonathan Ogden, Ray Lewis, Kevin Hardy, and Marvin Harrison— but the Jets were locked in on one player: Keyshawn Johnson.

Johnson had been a dominating receiver at the University of Southern California, where he twice became an All-American

Keyshawn Johnson smiles during a game against the Patriots on December 27, 1998. Johnson took some heat for coming to the Jets with an attitude and subsequently publishing a book where he impugned his teammates' abilities.

selection. After leading the Trojans to a win in the 1995 Cotton Bowl, Johnson was named the game's Most Valuable Player, and the following season he earned the same honor in the Rose Bowl when he caught 12 passes for 216 yards and a touchdown. USC won both games, and Johnson cemented his legacy at the football powerhouse.

In making Johnson the top pick of the draft, the Jets became the first team to select a receiver with the top pick since 1984, when the New England Patriots selected Irving Fryar. But even Johnson's presence did little to improve the Jets in his rookie season, as they posted a 1–15 record. Still, Johnson established himself as a the go-to receiver, hauling in 63 passes for 844 yards and eight touchdowns during his rookie season.

Better times were ahead for Johnson and the Jets. After the 1996 season, head coach Rich Kotite lost his job and Bill Parcells came on board for the 1997 season.

Things quickly began to change for the Jets, and Johnson played an integral role in the winning that followed once Parcells took charge. Not only could Johnson catch the football, he also brought an unseen tenacity to blocking, and he hungered to win. All perfect attributes for Parcells football.

Neil O'Donnell took over full-time at quarterback, often finding Johnson, who hauled in 70 passes for 963 yards, and the Jets effectively turned around the franchise by going 9–7 in Parcells' first season.

Vinny Testaverde came on board to quarterback the Jets in 1998, further improving the offense. And Johnson thrived, catching 83 passes for 1,131 yards and a career-high 10 touchdowns. The Jets stormed into the playoffs with a 12–4 record that season. After a bye week, the AFC East champions faced the Jacksonville Jaguars at the Meadowlands on January 10, 1999, in a divisional playoff game.

Johnson could not be stopped that day. He caught a 21-yard strike from Testaverde in the first quarter to put the Jets up 7–0, and in the second quarter he ran for a 10-yard touchdown to put the Jets up 17–0. Johnson finished with nine catches for 121 yards that day as the Jets took a 34–24 win.

One win away from advancing to the Super Bowl, the Jets lost 23–10 to the Broncos the following week in Denver to end their season.

Johnson turned in another stellar effort in 1999 when he caught 89 passes for 1,170 yards and eight touchdowns for the 8–9 Jets. But that season would be his last with the team.

The Jets traded Johnson to the Tampa Bay Buccaneers on April 12, 2000, in return for two first round-draft choices in the 2000 NFL Draft. The Jets would use those picks to select Shaun Ellis and Anthony Becht.

After the trade, Johnson signed an eight-year, $56 million contract extension with the Bucs that gave him the most expensive contract in the NFL for a wide receiver.

Johnson gained a Super Bowl ring in 2002 while playing with the Bucs, but his tenure in Tampa did not end well after Bucs coach Jon Gruden and he had a dispute that led to Johnson being traded to Dallas.

Johnson finished his career playing for the Carolina Panthers in 2006.

42 Brett Favre

Throughout the Jets' history, they have seemingly been infatuated with quarterbacks who played college football in the South. Joe Namath, Richard Todd, Browning Nagle....

At no time in the organization's history was this infatuation more apparent than in 2008 when they made a play for future Hall of Fame quarterback Brett Favre.

Favre had been the starting quarterback at the University of Southern Mississippi for four years when the Atlanta Falcons selected him in the second round of the 1991 NFL Draft. What happened next became an NFL fairy tale—for the Green Bay Packers.

When the Falcons looked at Favre, they didn't see a franchise player, much less a quarterback who could lead their team. So after one season, they traded him to the Packers for the 19th pick of the 1992 NFL Draft, which turned out to be the worst trade in Falcons history.

Favre spent the next 18 seasons as the gunslinging quarterback and leader of the Packers. Twice he led the Packers to the Super Bowl, leading them to a win over the New England Patriots in Super Bowl XXXI before losing the following year to the Denver Broncos in Super Bowl XXXII.

Along the way, Favre won three consecutive Associated Press Most Valuable Player Awards while leading the Packers to seven division championships. After the 2007 season—a season that saw Favre lead the Packers to the playoffs with a 13–3 record—the record-setting quarterback announced that he had decided to retire on March 4, 2008, prompting the Packers to make plans for life after Favre. Problems came when Favre began to waver on his decision. In the spring of 2008, Favre decided he wanted to play again, which put the Packers in an awkward situation. They had already decided to go another direction with their team by committing to Aaron Rodgers as their new quarterback, which led them to a point where they had to either forget those plans and bring back Favre or stick to them and watch Favre go elsewhere.

Following a summer's worth of speculation about whether Favre really intended to play and what the Packers intended to do if he did decide to play, Favre filed for reinstatement with the NFL on July 29. Shortly thereafter he met with the Packers, and the meeting culminated in both parties agreeing that the time had come for them to part.

Rampant speculation about Favre's ultimate destination dominated sports discussions in the days that followed before the Jets acquired him for a conditional fourth-round pick in the NFL Draft with performance escalation.

Initially the move appeared to be a godsend for the Jets' fortunes. Favre got the Jets off to an 8–3 start, which included a six-touchdown performance against the Arizona Cardinals. But the season did not end well. The Jets dropped four of their final five games. In those games he threw just two touchdowns while getting intercepted eight times. Particularly painful for Jets fans had been the loss in the final game of the season against the Miami Dolphins, when former Jets quarterback Chad Pennington—who was released to accommodate Favre—led the Dolphins' attack.

In fairness to Favre, an MRI in late December that season revealed a torn biceps tendon in his right shoulder, which led to his announcing his second retirement from football in February 2009.

Favre continued to belong to the Jets until he was released in April 2009, and after another summer's worth of speculation about whether Favre indeed was finished, he signed a contract to play for the Minnesota Vikings in 2009.

Favre's final chapter with the Jets came in the form of a fine to the tune of $125,000 that the NFL slapped on the Jets for being aware that Favre had been injured during the 11th game of the 2008 season and not reporting the injury.

Shoulder surgery took care of Favre's physical restriction, and he thrived for the Vikings in 2009, leading the team to the NFL Championship Game, where the Vikings lost in overtime to the New Orleans Saints.

Fortunately for the Jets, Mark Sanchez arrived on the scene prior to the 2009 season, which limited the thinking about what might have been had the Jets had a healthy Favre for an entire season.

43 Watch the Joe Namath and Farrah Fawcett Commercial

Talk about the meeting of two pop-culture icons, how about the Noxzema commercial that aired during the early 1970s that featured Joe Namath and Farrah Fawcett?

Of course, everybody knew who Namath was at the time, while nobody knew who Fawcett was, which did little to distract from the fact that she fulfilled her part for the commercial as the gorgeous blonde who had Namath's complete attention during a foamy shave. The tagline for the suggestive ad was, "Let Noxzema cream your face."

During the commercial, Fawcett sings, "Let Noxzema cream your face" while she applies shaving cream to Namath's smiling mug. At the beginning of the ad, Namath sheepishly notes, "I'm so excited! I'm gonna get creamed!"

At the end of the ad, when Fawcett nestles her face close to Namath's, he smiles and tells Fawcett, "You've got a great pair of hands." Fawcett would go on to become an American icon.

She appeared in many commercials during the late 1960s and 1970s for products other than Noxzema, including Wella Balsam shampoo, Mercury Cougar, and Ultra Brite toothpaste, which led to TV parts in *I Dream of Jeannie*, *Owen Marshall: Counselor at Law*, and *The Six Million Dollar Man*.

Early in 1976, two events coincided with one another that would turn Fawcett into a lasting icon from 1970s pop culture.

First, a poster of a smiling Fawcett wearing a red bathing suit went into production and came out at approximately the same time she played Jill Munroe in a TV movie that launched a series that fall titled *Charlie's Angels*, which also starred Jaclyn Smith and Kate

Jackson as private investigators working for Charles Townsend, a multimillionaire none of the women had ever met.

Fawcett was candid in a *TV Guide* interview about the show's popularity when she said, "When the show was number three, I thought it was our acting. When we got to be number one, I decided it could only be because none of us wears a bra."

The TV show's popularity sent the sales of her poster into orbit with estimates of poster sales in the area of 12 million. Meanwhile, her unique hairstyle became the rage for women all over the country, who wanted to imitate the style that had all the guys drooling. Fawcett became a national obsession overnight.

She left the *Charlie's Angels* series after just one season, and the show remained on the air another five years, enjoying great success.

Fawcett would go on to star in movies later in her career, but she never reached the acclaim she did while filling the airwaves during the 1970s.

She did receive a lot of attention at the end of her life when she and a friend filmed her day-to-day life while she coped with her fight against anal cancer. The result came in a documentary titled *Farrah's Story* that aired a little more than a month before her death on June 25, 2009, and was watched by over 9 million viewers.

44 Take Time to Root Against Bill Belichick

If a public enemy No. 1 exists for the Jets, one man fits the bill: Bill Belichick.

Even if the day comes when Belichick leaves his post as head coach of the New England Patriots to coach another team, the inclination to cheer against any team associated with Belichick should come as naturally to a Jets fan as cheering against the Red Sox if you're a Yankees fan.

Yes, Belichick is brilliant. And yes, he's one of the best coaches in the history of the National Football League. But he has been a constant pain in the posterior for Jets fans since the day he arrived in New York in 1970 to begin a 12-year tenure with the New York Giants.

For most Jets fans, the fact that Belichick spent that amount of time in the Giants organization is enough to make their Joe Namath throwback jerseys come unraveled. But adding to that fact that he actually served on the Giants' staff and helped the team win two Super Bowls brings more reasons to dislike the football savant.

Belichick coached well enough while with the Giants to land the head coaching job with the Cleveland Browns, where he did not last long before reuniting with Bill Parcells in New England. Once Parcells moved on to the Jets, Belichick followed his mentor and coached for the good guys for three seasons, serving as the Jets' assistant head coach and defensive coordinator from 1997 to 1999. The time he spent on the Jets' sideline only created the opening for Belichick to commit his most heinous act against the J-E-T-S!

As Bill Parcells was partial to doing, he retired as the Jets' head coach after the 1999 season. Belichick became the natural successor as the new leader of the team, and the move was announced in January 2000 that he would indeed assume the role as head coach for the 2000 season. But the Giants blue in Belichick came out when he resigned before he ever really got going. Belichick ended up coaching the Patriots, who had to cough up a first-round draft pick to gain the rights to hire him.

No first-round pick was worth what Belichick would have brought to the Jets' sideline. Making matters worse, Belichick's

Moe Lewis' Fateful Hit

Moe Lewis played linebacker for the Jets from 1991 through 2003 and created one of his more lasting memories for the Jets—and the New England Patriots—in the second game of the 2001 season.

The Jets traveled to New England to meet the Patriots on September 23, 2001, and the defense came to play that day, keeping talented Patriots quarterback Drew Bledsoe in check the entire game. By the time the fourth quarter rolled around, the Jets maintained a 10–3 lead.

With approximately five minutes left in the game, the Patriots faced a third-and-10 from their 19. After Bledsoe took the snap, he once again saw all of his men covered, so he tried to make a play and took off running. Lewis saw the Patriots' quarterback coming his way, and when he did not slide, the veteran linebacker lowered the boom on Bledsoe right in front of the Patriots bench.

Bledsoe felt the hit and remained on the ground after the play. Patriots personnel tended to Bledsoe as he remained on the ground for two minutes before finally heading toward the nearby sideline.

Somehow Bledsoe managed to return to the Patriots huddle on their next series, but Patriots coach Bill Belichick recognized something was wrong, so he lifted Bledsoe from the game and inserted a little-known quarterback by the name of Tom Brady.

Bledsoe ended up being taken to Massachusetts General Hospital via ambulance while Brady seemed to give his team a little spark, leading the Patriots to the Jets' 29 on their final drive of the game before throwing four incomplete passes to end the game.

The Jets won the game 10–3, the Patriots fell to 0–2, and their quarterback sat in the hospital with a tube in his chest to help reduce the internal bleeding.

Brady had been selected by the Patriots in the sixth round of the 2000 NFL Draft and played in just one game in 2000 before beating out Damon Huard for the Patriots' backup spot in training camp prior to the 2001 season.

Though Lewis' hit had been the kind defensive coaches praise, the end result was not good for the Jets or their fans.

Bledsoe, who had missed just six of 130 games to that point in nine NFL seasons, would be sidelined a couple of weeks. And Brady would be getting his opportunity.

"I've always told myself to be ready for the opportunity, because you never know how many you're going to get," Brady said.

You could say Brady made the most of his opportunity.

The Patriots thrived with Brady running their offense, and they beat the Jets 17–16 in their next meeting in 2001 en route to a run that would take them to the Super Bowl, where they would upset the St. Louis Rams.

Patriots played the Jets twice a year, usually serving up reminders on both occasions about why Belichick should live in infamy with Jets fans.

Belichick's Patriots lost the first three games he coached against the Jets before the Patriots won their second meeting during the 2001 season, thereby heading off on a tear that saw the Patriots win 12 of their next 14 regular-season meetings, which also included the September 9, 2007, contest that came to be known as Spygate after the NFL caught the Patriots videotaping the Jets' defensive signals. Subsequently, Belichick received a $500,000 fine.

While the fine proved to be the largest imposed on a coach in league history, had Jets fans issued the fine, it might have been tripled.

Thus, Jets fans need to collectively pull against Belichick no matter what the endeavor—from coaching the Patriots to playing in a charity golf event. The brilliant coach could have brought a dynasty to the Jets, but he chose to do so elsewhere.

45 Thomas Jones Sets Jets Rushing Mark

Thomas Jones set the new Jets rushing record on October 18, 2009, but it was the run that was called back—and would have added to Jones' new mark—that will be remembered as most significant on that historic day against the Buffalo Bills.

Jones arrived on the Jets in 2007 as a seasoned and tough NFL running back. He'd played for the Arizona Cardinals, Tampa Bay Buccaneers, and Chicago Bears before the Jets acquired him by simply dropping 26 spots in the 2007 NFL Draft. By doing so, the Bears received the 36th overall selection, while the Jets received Jones and the 63rd selection.

The strategy paid off well for the Jets, who got from Jones what they hoped they would when they acquired him.

Jones gained 1,119 yards for the Jets in 2007, then rushed for 1,312 yards and scored 14 touchdowns in 2008—a season for which he gained his first career trip to the Pro Bowl.

Once the 2009 season rolled around, Jones discovered that he had company in the Jets' backfield with the arrival of Shonn Greene, whom the Jets had drafted out of Iowa. That didn't stop Jones from putting together another banner season that included his assault on Curtis Martin's club record of 203 rushing yards in a single game, a record Martin had set on December 3, 2000.

Jones' record-setting performance against the Bills came in the Jets' sixth game of the season when they hosted their in-state rivals at the Meadowlands.

Early in the second quarter Jones broke loose on a 71-yard touchdown jaunt that personified the day he would have along with the kind of rushing day the Jets' offense had that afternoon as the team rushed for 318 yards.

Despite the Jets' ground success, the game stood tied at 13 at the end of regulation, sending the game into overtime. During overtime, the Jets faced a third-and-5 at the Bills' 23. That's when Jones broke away for an 11-yard gain, which appeared to be his most important carry of the afternoon because of what it could have led to for the Jets. Unfortunately for the Jets, the officials called a holding penalty on the play, which eventually put the Jets in a situation where they needed a long field goal to win the game, rather than a chip shot. The end result came wrapped in a 16–13 defeat to the Bills, which could be largely attributed to Mark Sanchez's five interceptions. Losing the game took the luster away from the fact that Jones had established a new team record of 210 yards on 22 carries. Given Jones' team-first mentality, the record proved to be a hollow experience due to the game's outcome.

"We didn't win the game," Jones said. "Regardless of my individual statistics, it doesn't matter."

Jones finished the season with 1,402 yards, to give him three consecutive 1,000 rushing seasons while with the Jets.

Jones' parting shot with the Jets came during the team's 17–14 divisional playoff win at San Diego when he iced the game with a two-yard gain on fourth-and-1 with just over a minute remaining.

Not only did Jones perform for the Jets, he also provided a solid presence in the clubhouse. The Jets released Jones in the spring of 2010; he then signed a two-year deal with the Kansas City Chiefs.

46 High Hopes End in Miami

Years of work seemed to be coming together for the Jets during the strike-shortened 1982 season.

Richard Todd had finally begun to live up to his promise in 1981 when the Jets went 10–5–1 and made the playoffs. Even though they lost 31–27 to the Buffalo Bills in the AFC Wild-Card Game, hopes were high for the 1982 season. And despite the players' strike that cost the Jets a portion of their season, they managed to pull things together and finish with a record of 6–3 to make the playoffs for the second consecutive year.

Walt Michaels had a team that included 36 players drafted by the Jets, and they seemed to be maturing nicely as the team entered the playoffs.

After defeating the Cincinnati Bengals 44–17 in the AFC Wild-Card Game, the Jets disposed of the Los Angeles Raiders 17–14 in their division playoff game, putting them into the AFC Championship Game against the Miami Dolphins on January 23, 1983, in Miami.

The Jets had a balanced offense run by Todd, who had seemingly matured to run the attack that boasted of exceptional weapons in receiver Wesley Walker, who had caught 15 passes in the previous two playoff games, and Freeman McNeil, who had rushed for 202 yards against the Bengals and 101 against the Raiders. On defense, they ran a 4-3 lead by standout linebacker Lance Mehl and a famed pass rush by their front four.

Unfortunately for the Jets, they were meeting a team in the Dolphins that had beaten them twice during the regular season. Conversely, under Michaels, the Jets carried a 7–4–1 record against Don Shula's Dolphins.

Quarterback David Woodley led the Dolphins' attack that utilized two quality running backs in fullback Andra Franklin and halfback Tony Nathan.

The matchup between Jets offensive coordinator Joe Walton and Dolphins defensive coordinator Bill Arnsparger received much of the attention heading into the game. Both had been anointed

Take That, Miami

Rex Ryan is a lightning rod for controversy, whether he's on the Jets' sideline or not.

During the off-season following the 2009 season, Ryan attended a "Strikeforce Miami" mixed martial arts event at the BankAtlantic Center in Sunrise, Florida. During Showtime's broadcast of the event, the Jets' head coach got introduced to the crowd, which brought a ringing chorus of boos.

Ryan did not back down from the boisterous crowd, cutting the figure of part NFL coach, part championship wrestler. He addressed the beer-fueled crowd by telling them, "I'd like to thank everybody here in Miami. I know they love me. I want to just tell everybody in Miami, hey, we're coming to beat you twice next year."

Obviously, Ryan's remarks did not curb the crowd's...let's say "enthusiasm"...toward him. Eventually every man has a breaking point, and the Jets' coach had his that night. Once he'd heard enough, he expressed himself to the booing crowd by flipping them the dreaded bird, a gesture Jets defensive end Shawn Ellis was not surprised to see his coach deliver.

"He's one of those guys who, if you come at me, I'm coming at you," Ellis said. "It was all in fun. They were probably yelling and talking stuff at him, and it ticked him off. Fans can be like that."

Earlier in the 2009 season, Tennessee owner Bud Adams received a substantial fine of $250,000 for making the same gesture at a game, so Ryan's gesture could not go unpunished by the NFL, which fined him $50,000.

Ryan apologized

"It was stupid and inappropriate," Ryan said. "I wouldn't accept that type of behavior from one of the coaches or players, and it's unacceptable from me. I apologize to the Jets organization, the National Football League, and NFL fans everywhere."

No doubt Ryan fanned the flames of an already piping-hot rivalry.

with coaching-genius status for the magic they had worked on their respective sides of the ball.

By halfway through the third quarter, Arnspargers's troops had won the battle by holding the Jets scoreless as the Dolphins held a 7–0 lead on a soggy field. The Jets took over at their own 22 with just under four minutes to play in the third quarter, then proceeded to gain four yards on the first two plays of the series. On third down, Walker—who worked against double coverage for most of the day—found himself open by the right sideline. Todd spotted Walker and threw. Dolphins linebacker A.J. Duhe stepped in front of the pass, bobbled it before gaining control of the football, then ran 35 yards for the touchdown that literally put the game on ice.

Todd never looked comfortable playing in the prevailing conditions, which showed in his passing line. He completed just 15 of 37 passes that day for only 103 yards while throwing five interceptions. Duhe hauled in three of the interceptions.

The Dolphins took a 14–0 win, giving them the first shutout in an AFC Championship Game since the Dolphins defeated the Baltimore Colts 21–0 in 1971.

The Jets would not reach the Super Bowl for the second time in team history as the Dolphins made the trip to Pasadena to play the Washington Redskins in Super Bowl XVII.

47 Wahoo McDaniel

In 1964 when the Jets moved from the Polo Grounds to Shea Stadium, the team needed a player to step forward to become a fan favorite they could embrace.

Wahoo McDaniel was part Choctaw-Chickasaw Native American and was a fierce competitor on the field. His gig moonlighting as a professional wrestler eventually became his full-time occupation.

That player didn't necessarily have to be the most talented or engaging, he just needed to be someone they could relate to and a guy they wanted to push through the turnstiles to see play.

Out of nowhere that player materialized in the form of Edward "Wahoo" McDaniel.

McDaniel hailed from Bernice, Oklahoma, where he received his nickname from his father, who was known as "Big Wahoo."

Though he was born in Louisiana, McDaniel moved around between Texas and Oklahoma, where his father worked as a welder in the oil business. Translated, *Wahoo* meant "wrong hole" in Choctaw, so his name had applications in the oil business as well as the game of football.

A part Choctaw-Chickasaw Native American, McDaniel played college football at the University of Oklahoma, where he played linebacker for legendary coach Bud Wilkinson and earned a reputation as a hell-raiser due to his propensity for missing classes and drinking.

Leaving college, McDaniel went to the newly formed Houston Oilers of the American Football League in 1960. He spent a year in Houston before heading to the Denver Broncos. Prior to the 1964 season, the Broncos traded McDaniel to the Jets, and there, under the lights of Shea Stadium in the team's first game at the shiny new stadium, a star was born.

At least a star New York fans could relate to with their adoration.

The date was September 12, 1964, and the game, which was the Jets' first at Shea, was played on a Saturday night against the Broncos. On that night, McDaniel took vengeance on his former teammates by making 10 tackles and knocking down two passes in the Jets' 30–6 win. Accompanying McDaniel's feats was an echo from the stands that grew louder as the night went on: "Wahoo! Wahoo!"

Having discovered McDaniel, the Jets' faithful began to learn more about their hero, which only served to endear him further to their hearts because few in the history of the franchise were as colorful.

Among the more colorful aspects of McDaniel's life was the fact that he moonlighted as a professional wrestler, where he was known on the circuit as "Chief Wahoo McDaniel," and his signature move was, predictably, the "Indian Tomahawk Chop," which he used like a weapon to finish off opponents.

Since those days, the sporting public has grown to recognize that professional wrestling is a staged production, which was true in McDaniel's day as well. But that didn't take anything away from the accompanying dangers of participating in the sport. McDaniel sported a scar across his stomach as a result of getting gored by one of the horns on opposing wrestler the Viking's helmet. Thirty-six stitches were required to close the wound.

McDaniel played just two years for the Jets before the Dolphins selected him in the AFL's expansion draft in 1966. He spent three years with the Dolphins before he got traded to the San Diego Chargers in the aftermath of a fight with police officers.

McDaniel never played for the Chargers. Instead he transitioned to a full-time career in professional wrestling, where he enjoyed great popularity as one of the "good guys" fighting the forces of evil, such as Boris Malenko. He would go on to have celebrated feuds in the ring with Johnny Valentine, "Superstar" Billy Graham, and Ric Flair, all of which served to make McDaniel far more of a legend in wrestling circles than in professional football.

While McDaniel never amounted to much in professional football, he clearly reigned as one of the early favorites for the growing legions of Jets fans.

48 Join a Jets Fan Club

If you're a Jets fan, there's no reason to hide your allegiance, which translates to meeting with others to root for the team you love, the Jets. And that means joining a Jets fan club.

Yeah, joining a Jets fan club might sound a little high schoolish on the surface, but doing so can be a lot of fun, and you don't have to live in the New Jersey–New York area to do so.

Once you decide that joining a club would indeed enhance your life, the first move should be checking out the Jets website at http://www.newyorkjets.com

Many things can be found at this website regarding all things New York Jets. For starters, you can find a Jets club in your area.

At the home page, click on the "Fanzone," which will bring up several subheads, one of which is "Out of Town Fans." Click that, and it will navigate you toward a directory that says, "Show me fan clubs in."

That is where you will scroll to the state in which you live. For example, if you live in Tampa, Florida, you will find the New York Jets Fan Club of Tampa along with the description, "We are a growing group of Jets fans who live in and around the Tampa, FL area and meets for every NY Jets game at Peabody's billiards."

In addition, contact information is given for joining the group.

Again, using the Tampa example, wouldn't you rather sit around with other Jets fans on a Sunday afternoon watching the Jets and talking about your favorite team instead of being stuck at home watching the Tampa Bay Buccaneers? Even worse, you could be sitting out in the heat at Raymond James Stadium watching the Bucs when you could be watching Jets football with others who bleed the same shade of green as you.

Jets fans are unique. So Jets fans getting acquainted with other Jets fans is an easy exercise due to the common denominator of their love of the Jets. In essence, if you're new to a city, utilizing the local Jets clubs to make friends is the way to go.

In addition, by going to the website, Jets fans can also find fan-friendly Jets bars in their locale. These are places that normally show the Jets games on Sundays and where Jets fans can mingle with other Jets fans.

Gang Green has plenty of fans all over the country, so unite and get to know one another by joining your local Jets fan club.

49 Joe Klecko

Joe Klecko wasn't the marquee act of the Jets' famed Sack Exchange, but No. 73 clearly was the backbone.

Mark Gastineau received most of the kudos for the Jets' front four of the late 1970s and early 1980s, as he got the most sacks and possessed the most attention-grabbing antics of the group.

Klecko brought a nice counterbalance to Gastineau's glitz.

After attending Temple University, Klecko joined the Jets when they drafted him in the sixth round of the 1977 NFL Draft with the 144th pick of the draft. He brought with him a toughness that could be defined in what he did when he wasn't playing football for Temple.

For starters, he boxed and twice won the NCAA club boxing title in the heavyweight division. And what would you expect a kid who loved football to do when he wasn't playing football? How about playing more football? That's right, Klecko secretly played semipro football for the Aston Knights using the name of Jim Jones to keep his college eligibility.

That desire and toughness fueled Klecko throughout his career in the NFL.

Klecko initially played defensive end, and together with Gastineau, Abdul Salaam, and Marty Lyons formed a front that managed to sack the quarterback 66 times in 1981.

He would go on to become a Pro Bowl selection in 1981, 1983, 1984, and 1985, and he made All-Pro in 1981 and 1985.

In 1985 the Jets went to a 3-4 defense, and Bud Carson, the team's defensive coordinator, asked Klecko to move to nose tackle to accommodate the change from a four-man front. He did so without complaint, even though he had never played the position in the past.

Before his playing days were over, Klecko would play end, tackle, and nose tackle on the front line. While doing so, he earned the distinction of becoming the first player in professional football history to be selected to the Pro Bowl at three different positions.

Jets fans adored Klecko, and opponents respected him for who he was and for his ability.

"In my 13 seasons, Joe is right there at the top of the defensive ends I had to block, up there with Fred Dean, Lee Roy Selmon, and Bruce Smith. Joe was the strongest guy I ever faced," Hall of Fame tackle Anthony Munoz told the *New York Times*. "He had perfect technique—hands in tight, great leverage. My second year, 1981, we went to Shea and beat the Jets 31–30, but he was such an intense, smart player, I knew I was in a battle. He was the leader, the guy who kept that unit together."

Hall of Fame guard Joe DeLamielleure told the *New York Times*, "I had to block Joe Greene and Merlin Olsen when I was playing and, believe me, Joe Klecko was equal to those two guys. If Joe Klecko had played one position for 10 years, he'd have been considered one of the top two or three players at that position, whichever one it was. There's not another player who went to the Pro Bowl at three different positions. You take a defensive end and put him at nose tackle, and he's just as good there, that's a great player."

Klecko played 12 seasons in the NFL, wearing the uniform of the Indianapolis Colts in his final season of 1988.

The Jets honored Klecko on December 26, 2004, by retiring his No. 73 jersey during a halftime ceremony, making him just the third Jet to have his number retired as he joined Hall of Famers Joe Namath and Don Maynard.

50 Marino's Fake Spike

The 1994 season began with promise when the Jets took wins at Buffalo against the Bills and against the Denver Broncos at the Meadowlands.

Dashing new coach Pete Carroll appeared up to the task of calling the shots in the AFC's Eastern Division, and he had veteran quarterback Boomer Esiason leading the charge. However, after the quick start, the team lost three straight to the Miami Dolphins, Chicago Bears, and Cleveland Browns, which set the tone for the season as they struggled to get back to .500 and remain in the division race.

By the time the Dolphins came to the Meadowlands on November 27, the Jets had seemingly righted their ship with a record of 6–5, and they were back in the thick of things in the division as the Dolphins entered the game with a record of 7–4. So a win at home would move the Jets into a tie for first place with four games remaining on the schedule.

Jets fans smelled the postseason, and seemingly so did the Jets, who led 17–0 early in the third quarter on a Nick Lowery field goal, an Esiason touchdown pass to Johnny Mitchell, and a three-yard touchdown run by Brad Baxter.

Miami quarterback Dan Marino finally answered by throwing a 10-yard touchdown pass to Mark Ingram, but a two-point attempt failed, which made the score 17–6.

Esiason held the team together and calmly led the Jets back up the field to the Dolphins' 10 before again hitting Mitchell to build a 24–6 cushion for the Jets late in the third quarter.

For all intents and purposes, the Jets appeared to have the game on ice.

But Marino connected with Ingram for a second touchdown pass before the third quarter concluded and he hit Irving Fryar on the two-point conversion to cut the Jets' lead to 24–14 entering the fourth quarter.

Suddenly the Jets' offense went in the tank while Marino seemed to be just getting warmed up.

The future Hall of Fame Dolphins quarterback again hit Ingram for a 28-yard touchdown to cut the lead to 24–21.

Again, the Jets could not get anything going on offense, which allowed the Dolphins to have the ball at the end of the game. Marino took advantage of the situation by driving his team to the Jets' 8 with approximately 30 seconds on the clock, which continued to run.

That's when Marino's backup Bernie Kozar's voice filled the speaker inside his helmet telling him to run the clock play at Jets rookie cornerback Aaron Glenn. Marino agreed with the call and glanced Ingram's way, which was the veteran quarterback's way of telling his receiver the play; Ingram would figure it out.

With everybody in the Meadowlands believing that Marino would take the snap then spike the football to stop to clock to set up a game-tying field goal by Pete Stoyanovich, Marino threw everyone for a loop. After taking the snap, he faked like he would be spiking the football, and Glenn took the bait. Marino's pass hit Ingram in the gut for his fourth touchdown of the game.

Suddenly the Dolphins were leading for the first time in the game by a score of 28–24, and the Meadowlands had grown quiet in the realization that what appeared to be an uplifting victory had suddenly turned into a devastating defeat.

Having suffered a severe change in momentum, the Jets lost their final four games of the season to finish at 6–10. Pete Carroll got fired after one season on the job, and the Dolphins went on to win the AFC East division with a record of 10–6.

51 Last Team Standing

Bruce Coslet's four-year tenure as Jets coach hardly instilled the fiber Lombardi once did while coaching the Packers to countless successes. However, his teams did have their moments, such as the regular-season finale against the Dolphins on December 22, 1991.

Mediocre football in the AFC East had enabled the Jets to remain in the postseason hunt. They entered the last week of the season with a 7–8 record as they traveled to Miami to—as most felt—put the lid on another season of uninspiring football against their division rival, the 8–7 Dolphins, coached by Don Shula.

The funny part of the equation came in the fact that even though the Jets should have been out of contention, they weren't, and a scenario came into being that the winner of the Jets-Dolphins game would become the final wild-card team and advance to the playoffs.

Indeed, the Jets had a chance at making the playoffs, but Coslet's troops had dropped successive games to the Buffalo Bills, Detroit Lions, and New England Patriots before heading to Miami. So any belief that the Jets might rise from the ashes appeared to be something from a fairy tale.

Ken O'Brien had become the most popular target of the fans as the Jets quarterback had thrown just 10 touchdown passes during the season. Accompanying the despair of O'Brien's playing ability were questions of whether he would be back with the Jets the following season, a question that seemed far-fetched given what had been forecast for him when he joined the team five years earlier. Conversely, Dolphins quarterback Dan Marino entered the contest, having thrown 23 touchdowns, many of them landing in the dependable hands of receivers Mark Clayton and Mark Duper.

On the bright side, the unpredictable Jets were facing an unstable Dolphins squad that had blown a 13-point lead the previous week by allowing the San Diego Chargers to score 28 points in the final quarter of the game. And for some reason, O'Brien always seemed to be at his best against the Dolphins as he carried a 61.7 percent completion percentage into the game with 21 touchdowns in his career against the Dolphins.

Clayton had been outspoken for the Dolphins the week of the game, boldly declaring that his team would take care of the Jets handily. The declaration began to look silly once the game began and the Jets took a 7–0 lead on Brad Baxter's one-yard run.

Clayton backed his mouth by hauling in an 18-yard touchdown pass from Marino in the second quarter, which took the game to the half tied at 7.

The Jets never wilted in a second half that saw the lead go back and forth until the Jets found themselves trailing 20–17 at their own 30 with 38 seconds remaining.

O'Brien played brilliantly in the drive that followed, hitting passes of 23 and 14 yards before throwing incomplete to stop the clock. With eight seconds remaining, Freeman McNeil took a handoff and ran seven yards before heading out of bounds. Two seconds were left on the clock when Jets kicker Raul Allegre entered the game and kicked a 44-yard field goal to send the game into overtime.

In the extra period, the Jets' defense bowed up to stop Marino, giving the ball back to O'Brien, who successfully mixed his passes with runs by Johnny Hector to get Allegre into field-goal range. He drilled a 30-yard field goal through the uprights, and the Jets had a 23–20 win.

Afterward, Jets players reflected on Clayton's words prior to the game.

"You don't say things like that," Hector told the *New York Times*. "It sparks teams. It definitely did us."

Added Jets safety Lonnie Young, "He's no Broadway Joe."

The Jets were in the playoffs for the first time since 1986—and Shula and the Dolphins were not.

Denying Shula a trip to the postseason might have been the most rewarding aspect of this win for many Jets fans. Shula's comments afterward warmed the souls of Jets fans everywhere when he said, "This is one that's going to last a long time with me. All of a sudden there's nowhere to go and nothing to do."

52 Forgive Ken O'Brien

Quality quarterbacks were in abundance for the 1983 NFL Draft.

If you were a team holding a first-round selection and needed a top-notch quarterback, chances were you would come away with a good one.

John Elway became the first selection when the Baltimore Colts grabbed the Stanford quarterback. Penn State's Todd Blackledge became the next quarterback taken when the Kansas City Chiefs picked seventh. Jim Kelly then went to the Buffalo Bills with the 14th pick and Tony Eason to the New England Patriots with the 15th.

Ken O'Brien throws a second-quarter pass under pressure from the Dolphins in this September 21, 1986, game at Giants Stadium.

The Jets wanted a quarterback, and the time for them to pick was drawing near. When the Dallas Cowboys used the 23rd pick of the first round to take defensive end Jim Jeffcoat, the Jets knew they would be able to get their man.

Jets fans figured that man would be Dan Marino, the record-setting quarterback from the University of Pittsburgh. He came from the state of Pennsylvania, just like Joe Namath, and he also had Broadway Joe's quick release. So Marino appeared to be a natural for the pick.

But the Jets crossed up everyone by taking Ken O'Brien, a 6'4",
210-pound, strong-armed quarterback from California-Davis.
Three picks later the Dolphins selected Marino, thereby forever
cursing O'Brien as the quarterback who would be remembered as
the guy the Jets took instead of Marino.

Fact is, O'Brien might not have been Marino, but he hardly
was a slouch.

To fully appreciate O'Brien, Jets fans must first look past the
fact that Marino could have worn the green and white. If you can
manage to get over that one, you will be better equipped to focus
on some of the positives accomplished by O'Brien during his nine
seasons with the Jets.

While with the Jets, O'Brien threw for almost 25,000 yards, a
plateau he would surpass in his final season in the NFL with the
Philadelphia Eagles in 1993. In 1985 he led the Jets to an 11–5
record and a trip to the playoffs; he also ranked as the top-rated
quarterback in the NFL that season.

Building on what he had helped the Jets accomplish in 1985,
O'Brien led the Jets to a 10–1 start in 1986 before breaking a finger,
which sent the team into a tailspin that saw them lose their final
five games. Despite the way the Jets finished the season, they still
managed to make the playoffs, and they defeated the Chiefs in the
wild-card game before bowing out to the Cleveland Browns.

Of note, during the 1986 season, O'Brien and Marino hooked
up in a memorable shootout on September 21 that saw O'Brien
throw for 479 yards and four touchdowns while Marino threw for
448 yards and six touchdowns in an overtime game the Jets won
51–45.

Jets coach Joe Walton put it this way when talking about
O'Brien in 1986: "I've been around a lot of tough, smart guys who
won even though they couldn't throw the football that well. Billy
Kilmer with the Redskins, Fran Tarkenton with the Giants, they
didn't have a lot of physical ability, they did it by being tough and

Smokin' Marino

Dan Marino will live forever as the guy the Jets didn't draft when they should have in the 1983 NFL Draft.

At no time did Jets fans have the chance to admire him more than when he became the enemy quarterback to throw for the most yardage in a single game against the Jets on October 23, 1988.

The nice part of the equation came in the fact that even though Marino set a standard that might never be broken, the Jets won the game 44–30 at Joe Robbie Stadium in Miami.

Ironically, everything had seemed to be going wrong for the Jets prior to the game. Mark Gastineau, the team's leading pass rusher, had just retired, the Jets had not won in Miami since 1980, and the Dolphins entered the game riding a three-game winning streak.

After the Jets stormed to a 30–10 halftime lead, the game got interesting.

Marino led the Dolphins to a 78-yard touchdown drive to start the second half that culminated with an 11-yard strike to Mark Clayton for six points.

When the Dolphins got the ball back, Marino directed the offense up the field again and found Jim Jensen for a two-yard touchdown pass. The extra point missed, leaving the Dolphins behind 37–23.

Marino's passes took the Dolphins 85 yards to another touchdown, which Troy Stradford finished off with a one-yard run, to cut the lead to 37–30 early in the fourth quarter.

The Dolphins quickly got the ball back and found themselves facing a fourth-and-1, at which point Dolphins coach Don Shula opted to have Tony Franklin try a 37-yard field goal, but the kick missed.

With just under four minutes remaining in the game, Jets defensive lineman Tom Baldwin pressured Marino and actually knocked the Miami quarterback off his feet, which upset his rhythm and allowed Rich Miano to make an interception for the Jets.

When all the smoke had cleared, Marino had completed 35 of 60 passes for 521 yards and three touchdowns—with five interceptions. In NFL history only Norm Van Brocklin had thrown for more yardage, as he accrued 554 yards through the air in 1951 while playing for the Los Angeles Rams.

smart. But in addition to being tough and smart, Kenny O'Brien can throw the football."

Another endearing O'Brien quality came in the fact that he could be downright miserly with interceptions, as evidenced by the fact that he had the lowest rate of interceptions in the NFL in 1985, 1987, and 1988. Finally, O'Brien twice went to the Pro Bowl while calling the signals for the Jets.

In retrospect, Ken O'Brien will never be mistaken for Dan Marino, but he turned out to be a pretty good player. So just maybe it's time Jets fans forgave him for not being Marino.

53 Memorable O'Brien– Marino Shootout

Not since Joe Namath and Johnny Unitas hooked up in a shootout in Baltimore had Jets fans seen anything like what happened on September 21, 1986. That's the day Ken O'Brien and Dan Marino went at each other in the Meadowlands like two gunslingers.

Both quarterbacks were in their prime, validated by the fact that Marino had been the NFL's top-ranked quarterback in 1984 and O'Brien the top-ranked quarterback in 1985. And the previous time the Jets and Dolphins had met on November 10, 1985, in Miami, the pair had put on an aerial display that saw them combine for over 700 yards passing in a 21–17 Jets loss in Miami.

O'Brien had passed for 393 yards that day and Marino 362, so the anticipation for what might happen was there. And the pair of quarterbacks, who were selected by their respective teams in the first round of the 1983 NFL Draft, did not disappoint.

Ironically, the first quarter of that affair proved rather sedate when compared to what was to come. The Jets got on the board first with a Pat Leahy field goal before Marino threw a six-yard touchdown pass to James Pruitt to put the Jets up 7–3 with three quarters to go.

The second quarter brought a different story as O'Brien and Marino began to fill the air with footballs.

O'Brien passed the Jets up the field on two drives to start the quarter that culminated with touchdown runs of one and eight yards by Johnny Hector.

Marino answered with touchdown passes of one yard to Dan Johnson and 13 yards to Mark Duper.

Not to be outdone, O'Brien finished out the second quarter with touchdown passes of 65 and 50 yards to Wesley Walker to give the Jets a 31–21 halftime advantage.

All told, six touchdowns were scored in the second quarter with neither defense giving any kind of indication that they might be able to stop one of the young quarterbacks in the second half.

Even though the Jets continued to move the ball behind O'Brien's passes, the third quarter belonged to the Dolphins, who got a field goal and two touchdown passes from Marino to Duper for 46 yards and Bruce Hardy for one to put the Dolphins up 38–31 with 15 minutes remaining.

O'Brien guided the Jets up the field at the start of the fourth quarter with a drive that culminated in Dennis Bligen's seven-yard touchdown run that tied the game. But Marino quickly connected with Mark Clayton on a four-yard touchdown, giving Marino six touchdown passes during the game and the Dolphins a 45–38 lead.

The Jets appeared to be out of time when they found themselves on the Dolphins' 21 with five seconds to go, but O'Brien would not be denied. When Miami cornerback Reyna Thompson missed his assignment by not bumping Walker at the line, the Jets' wide receiver found the open spaces, and O'Brien delivered a strike that Walker took to the end zone to tie the score at 45 and send the game into overtime.

Predictably, the first team that got the ball in overtime won. O'Brien punched the winning ticket by connecting with Walker on a 43-yard touchdown to give the Jets a 51–45 victory.

During the game, Marino completed 30 of 50 passes for six touchdowns and 448 yards, and O'Brien had completed 29 of 43 for four touchdowns and 479 yards. Combined, the pair had thrown for an astounding 884 yards.

"There were fireworks on both sides of the field," O'Brien told the *New York Times*. "The important thing is we won the game."

54. The Monday Night Miracle

Though the Jets did not make the playoffs in 2000, the team and their fans experienced one of the more exciting seasons in franchise history given the team's ability to come from behind to claim victory. And no comeback victory in franchise history could top the one that took place on October 23, 2000, which came to be known as the "Miracle at the Meadowlands."

Heading into their *Monday Night Football* contest against the Miami Dolphins at the Meadowlands, the Jets understood that the game would likely be a slugfest between two struggling offenses as they tried to do anything against two solid defenses.

Both teams were 5–1 for the season. The Jets ranked seventh in the league in yards allowed while the Dolphins ranked eighth. Of note, the Dolphins' defense had allowed just three touchdowns and six field goals in the 16 trips opposing teams had made inside their 20.

But what had appeared to be a close contest turned into an old-fashioned beatdown for the Dolphins.

Quarterback Jay Fielder could do no wrong hitting receivers Leslie Shepherd and Oronde Gadsden, while Miami's running backs ran freely though the Jets' defense. Meanwhile, the Dolphins' defense held the Jets' offense by forcing them to punt after three downs on their first five series of the game.

All of the above resulted in a 30–7 Dolphins lead entering the fourth quarter.

By then a national TV audience had surmised that Dolphins coach Dave Wannstedt was a genius and that Jets coach Al Groh had grave coaching deficiencies. While the 2000 Jets were a team that never surrendered even when faced with great odds, a 23-point deficit looked to be too much even for them, particularly considering the game Vinny Testaverde was having.

After three quarters, the Jets quarterback had thrown three interceptions while throwing for just 102 yards. And this was the guy Jets fans were hoping could bring his team back against a Dolphins defense that had not allowed more than 16 points in a game the entire season?

In the midst of the Jets having their heads handed to them on a silver platter, center Kevin Mawae began to offer some bravado on the Jets' sideline, telling his teammates, "We're not going out like this."

And the Jets did not go gently that good night.

Something mysterious and intangible suddenly clicked into place, and the Jets scored 23 unanswered points to tie the game at 30 after a 24-yard Testaverde–to–Wayne Chrebet touchdown pass. But the Dolphins' offense quickly came back to life to score a touchdown on a Fiedler bomb to put them back on top 37–30. Not to worry, the Jets had something up their sleeve, which came in a tackle-eligible play that saw Testaverde hook up with Jumbo Elliott for a three-yard touchdown with 42 seconds remaining to tie the score at 37 and send the game into overtime.

Marcus Coleman picked off his second pass of the game in overtime, and the Jets' offense moved the ball well enough to get John Hall in position to kick a 40-yard field goal. His kick split the uprights to complete the greatest comeback in team history.

All told, the Jets had scored 30 points in the fourth quarter, and Testaverde threw for 235 yards and four touchdowns in the final period.

55 Watch *C.C. and Company*

If you're laying around on a weekend afternoon, channel flipping from one destination to the next, and suddenly the title *C.C. and Company* pops up, slam on the brakes and tune in, for this is a must-see film for any Jets fan.

For starters, this 1970 classic stars Joe Namath as the leading character, C.C. Ryder, in this low-budget biker classic. Even though Namath is not wearing the green and white in the film, Jets fans are able to see Namath when he still had youth on his side. He has not even turned 30. Looking at him—and not judging the acting—you can understand why he was such a heartthrob, as his charisma comes across on the screen.

While C.C. is a rough-and-tumble biker, he is lovable because he cares about others and is a decent enough guy to want to rescue a damsel in distress. In this story line, she is Ann McCalley, played by Ann Margaret.

McCalley is caught in a bad way when two of C.C.'s buddies—Captain Midnight and Lizard—want to rape her after they come upon her on the side of the road in a broken-down limousine. Her

Namath's Acting Career

Joe Namath rose to acting fame in *C.C. and Company*, but he went on to act in other movies and on several TV shows as well.

Namath's other movie roles included *Norwood*, *Chattanooga Choo Choo*, *Avalanche Express*, and *Last Rebel*. He actually was nominated for a Golden Globe for Most Promising Newcomer: Male in 1971 for his work in *Norwood*.

Most of Namath's TV work took place in guest-starring roles, which included shows such as *Married with Children, The Brady Bunch, The Flip Wilson Show, Rowan and Martin's Laugh-In, The Dean Martin Show, The Simpsons, The A-Team, ALF*, and *The John Larroquette Show*.

Namath had a starring role in *The Waverly Wonders*, a short-lived sitcom in which he played a former pro basketball player who becomes a basketball coach and a history teacher.

Memorable among Namath's TV roles was his work as T.J. on *The A-Team*, which included one episode that saw him receive threats from NFL Hall of Fame running back Jim Brown. Another episode saw Namath take a punch from *A-Team* icon Mr. T.

Namath entertained thoughts of becoming a serious actor, which led to his working on the stage in summer-stock productions of *Fiddler on the Roof* and *Damn Yankees*. "Broadway Joe" did appear on Broadway as a cast replacement in *The Caine Mutiny Court Martial*. Other highlights included his work as a guest host on *The Tonight Show Starring Johnny Carson; The Joe Namath Show*, which he did with noted journalist Dick Schaap serving as cohost; and he served as part of the *Monday Night Football* team.

driver has gone for help, and C.C. is trying to fix the car when the problems begin. Initially, C.C. offers a sort of bemused expression, and you think he's going to give in to pressure from his peers before he decides that what they are planning to do just isn't cool.

It doesn't take long for the audience to gather that Namath made the right choice by not quitting his day job to flee New York City and the Jets for Hollywood. Still, this flick remains a lot of fun.

C.C. ends up with Ann and of course manages to bed her while also converting from chopper rider to a dirt-bike racer—naturally he makes a flawless transition. None of these developments sit well with C.C.'s old gang, which feels they have been double crossed. In order to get back at C.C., they kidnap Ann.

Moon is the leader of the gang and is played by William Smith, who knew how to play an imposing villain (see his role as Falconetti in the TV miniseries *Rich Man, Poor Man*), which sets up a classic good versus evil confrontation between C.C. and Moon. In order to free Ann, C.C. challenges Moon to a chopper race.

How many fans of NFL teams get to see the most famous player in their team's history take part in a chopper race? That's entertainment.

Predictably, C.C. takes the race after much toil, and Moon meets a hard end as he crashes and goes up in flames at the end of the race. In the confusion that follows, C.C. rides off with Ann.

Though *C.C. and Company* is the perfect movie for a lazy Sunday afternoon, you might wait the rest of your life to see a random showing of the movie, so your best bet to see it would be to order the DVD.

56 Playoff Romp Over Bengals

Walt Michaels' tenure as head coach reached a high point on January 9, 1983, when the Jets went to Cincinnati for the opening round of the playoffs.

In order for the Jets to reach the Super Bowl they knew they had to win three consecutive games in the AFC playoffs, beginning with their game against the Bengals that would be played at Riverfront Stadium.

For Michaels, the setting of the game brought some personal angst. He had played linebacker for 10 seasons for the Cleveland Browns under legendary coach Paul Brown, for whom the team was named. Brown had been the Bengals' original coach but had since assumed the role of Bengals vice president and general manager. Even though Brown wasn't coaching, Michaels had to feel his aura just by being in the neighborhood of his coaching mentor.

Helping to smooth over any intangibles Brown might have given the Bengals was the return of Joe Klecko to the Jets. In the second game of the 1982 season, the Jets' stalwart defensive end had injured his right patella tendon, and the injury had required surgery. But the Jets entered the game as underdogs to the AFC's defending champions.

Seemingly nothing could go right for the Jets in the early going, as the Bengals took a 14–3 first-quarter lead on Ken Anderson touchdown passes of 32 yards to Isaac Curtis and two yards to Dan Ross on their first two drives of the game. But the Jets quickly got busy in the second quarter.

Slightly over two minutes into the second quarter, halfback Freeman McNeil found Derrick Gaffney with a 14-yard touchdown pass to cut the Bengals' lead to 14–10. That touchdown gave the Jets the first seven points of a run that saw the team hang 20 unanswered points on the scoreboard.

Meanwhile the Jets' defense began to apply the much-needed pressure to Anderson, who could cut up any team with his pinpoint accuracy if he had the time to throw. The Jets threw a new wrinkle at the Bengals by alternating from their familiar four-man defensive front to a 3-4 defense. The resulting confusion seemed to keep Anderson and his line guessing, and by the end of the game the Jets' defense had sacked Anderson four times and picked off three of his passes.

Known primarily for their ability to rush the passer, the Jets' defense showed how they could stop a run as well as they smothered the Bengals' running attack, limiting them to 62 yards rushing that afternoon.

McNeil thrived, giving life to the Jets' running game with 202 yards on 21 carries, including a 20-yard touchdown early in the fourth quarter that put the Jets up 30–17. The Jets' running attack freed quarterback Richard Todd to have one of his better days as he completed 20 of the 28 passes he attempted and just one found the enemy's hands, and that one interception came on a deflection. Walker became the beneficiary of Todd's freedom, catching eight passes for 145 yards.

Darrol Ray's 98-yard interception return for a touchdown gave the Jets a 31–17 lead with approximately five minutes to go to put the game out of reach.

Dewayne Crutchfield added a one-yard touchdown run to complete the Jets' 44–17 win in what likely was the most dominating postseason performance in club history.

57 Keyshawn Rules Against Jacksonville

Keyshawn Johnson never had a problem expressing the confidence he had in his own abilities.

After his rookie season with the Jets in 1996—a season that saw the Jets go 1–15—the Jets' wide receiver came out with a book titled *Just Give Me the Damn Ball!* On the one hand, Johnson came off as pretty cocky based on the book's message, which was how much better the Jets would be if they leaned on him more. On the other hand, Johnson might have been justified in his claims. His performance for the Jets on January 10, 1999, in their playoff game against the Jacksonville Jaguars, served to validate Johnson's self-assuredness and get others to buy into him after watching one of the most well-rounded performances in NFL history.

Johnson enjoyed a terrific season in 1998, catching 83 passes for 1,131 yards and 10 touchdowns as the Jets earned a spot in the playoffs with a 12–4 record. Having captured the AFC East title, the Jets earned a bye the first week of the playoffs before they met Jacksonville at the Meadowlands for a divisional playoff game.

The first indication Johnson gave that he might have a special day came after a Curtis Martin fumble at the Jacksonville 22. Chris Hudson of the Jaguars snatched up the ball and tore off for the end zone, and he might have made it all the way had he not decided for some reason to attempt a lateral at midfield. The lateral went badly, and Johnson, who had given chase to Hudson, was there to grab the ball for the Jets.

"I don't think I'm slow, so I said, 'One thing I'm going to do is run,'" Johnson told the *New York Times*. "If they don't catch him, I'm going to make sure I catch him somewhere down the line. When he went to lateral the ball, someone batted it, and I was right there, but that comes from hustling. If you don't hustle, you never know. They may have the ball, and the game's in a whole other situation."

Martin could be counted on as the Jets player who most appreciated Johnson's effort on the play. Afterward, he told the *New York Times*, "Keyshawn's the man."

By regaining control of the football, the Jets managed to burn additional time off the clock after running 11 plays to set up a John Hall field goal that gave them a 17–0 lead.

That afternoon Johnson hauled in nine passes for 121 yards and a 21-yard touchdown, he ran the ball twice for 28 yards—including a fake handoff to Martin that turned into a reverse for

Johnson and a touchdown on a 10-yard end around—and he had some late-game defense.

The Jets held a 10-point lead late in the game, and the situation dictated that Jacksonville quarterback Mark Brunnell cut loose with a Hail Mary pass. If he could somehow connect, the Jaguars still had a remote chance of recovering an onside kick and kicking a long field goal to send the game into overtime.

Understanding that the situation might come down to a jump ball, the Jets opted to insert Johnson into the defensive secondary. Brunnell did as expected and heaved the ball deep downfield, prompting a pack of players to leap for the football. Johnson got his hands on the ball, and when the resulting chaos cleared, it became evident that the receiver-turned–defensive back had come down with the football as if he'd boxed off the boards to pull down a rebound.

Final score: Jets 34, Jaguars 24.

58 Freeman McNeil

Freeman McNeil might have never played for the Jets had it not been for one play that took place in his senior season at UCLA.

While another team probably would have taken McNeil later in the first round, the Jets would have gone for somebody else with the third overall pick of the 1981 NFL Draft.

Yes, McNeil had excelled while running out of the I formation for the Bruins, but questions were out there regarding whether he could catch the football. Backs that could catch the ball out of the backfield had always held far greater value to NFL teams. So that question about McNeil's pass-catching abilities hung in the air until UCLA played crosstown rival USC his senior year. In that game UCLA quarterback Jay Schroeder threw to McNeil after getting chased out of the pocket. The ball appeared as though it would be intercepted, but just at the last instant McNeil tipped the ball out of the waiting hands of the Trojans' defensive back. Other defenders arrived on the scene, prompting McNeil to tip the ball from one hand to the other. Once McNeil had the football in his possession, he tore down the field for a 58-yard touchdown.

So as lore would have it, McNeil's draft stock soared after that one play, and the Jets were fortunate that it did, as he turned out to be one of the best backs in club history.

Those in the Los Angeles area were hardly surprised by McNeil's status.

As a senior at Banning High in the Los Angeles suburb of Wilmington, McNeil could not be stopped while gaining 1,343 yards and averaging 8.1 yards per clip with 27 touchdowns. He was named L.A. City Player of the Year, which earned him visits from Ohio State and USC. But he ended up at UCLA, where he initially played behind Theotis Brown and later James Owens, who both would play in the NFL. The Bruins went to the I formation, and McNeil rushed for 1,105 yards his senior year, which earned him some recognition. He made some All-America teams but not the kind that Southern backs Herschel Walker and George Rogers were getting as they occupied the backfield spots on most teams.

McNeil's true recognition would come at the next level.

He gained 623 yards his rookie season, despite missing time to injury—and he still led the team in rushing. After deciding to play at a lower weight the following season, McNeil cut 15 pounds from his 211-pound frame and followed in 1982 with 786 yards—which led the NFL during the strike-shortened season—and he caught 16 passes for 187 yards.

The Jets made the playoffs in 1982 with a 6–3 record, putting them in a first-round wild-card game against the Cincinnati Bengals in Cincinnati on January 9, 1983. There at Riverfront Stadium, McNeil put on a running clinic by accruing 202 yards on 21 carries, including a 35-yard touchdown run in the Jets' 44–17 dismantling of the Bengals.

McNeil surpassed 1,000 yards for the first time in 1984 when he rushed for 1,070 on 229 carries.

To help out McNeil, the Jets began to run a lot of their offense out of the I formation, which allowed him to run freely as he had at UCLA.

During his career, he never averaged less than four yards per carry in any season, and he twice made the Pro Bowl and made first-team All-Pro in 1982.

McNeil retired after the 1992 season, a day before his 34th birthday, when he told reporters, "I played with my heart because that's the only way I knew how to play. And I live my life with my heart. I stand up for what I believe in and I feel good about my career."

McNeil spent his entire 12-year career with the Jets, finishing with 8,074 yards rushing, averaging 4.5 yards per carry, and scoring 38 touchdowns.

59 Gerry Philbin

Gerry Philbin proved to be one of the unheralded heroes of the Jets while playing nine seasons at defensive end, including a superlative season during the team's Super Bowl run in the 1968 season.

Philbin started at defensive tackle for four years at the University of Buffalo, earning second-team All-American honors as well as the All-American Academic Team before moving to the professional ranks.

The Jets selected him in the third round of the 1964 American Football League Draft (19th overall pick) as did the Detroit Lions in the third round of the 1964 National Football League Draft (33rd overall pick). Receiving far more interest from the Jets, Philbin elected to remain in the state of New York by signing a contract with the AFL's New York entrée.

Philbin instantly became a starter at defensive end in 1964 but missed time during his rookie season with a shoulder injury. He returned in 1965 and remained a regular throughout the remainder of his tenure with the Jets.

Though a consistent performer throughout his career, Philbin's best season came in 1968 when he recorded 14½ sacks, according to several reports (sacks did not become an official statistic until 1982), then led the charged-up Jets defense that included Verlon Biggs, John Elliott, and Al Atkinson in Super Bowl III. While they held the Baltimore Colts to just seven points in one of the biggest upsets in football history, the game belonged to Namath and the offense.

"We took for granted that it was just part of the game," Philbin told NewYorkJets.com. "The glamour always went to the offense, the quarterback, and at that time we had the most glamorized quarterback and football player in all of sports, and that was great. So it was tough for the defense."

Philbin continued to be bothered by shoulder problems throughout his career, but he showed a lot of heart by overcoming those problems and playing on many occasions. Despite missing time after injuring his shoulder in the 12th game of the 1969 season, he found a way to return to the Jets' defense in time for the team's playoff game against the Kansas City Chiefs, and he recorded two sacks of Chiefs quarterback Len Dawson.

Philbin twice made first-team All-Pro in addition to twice making the Pro Bowl, and he played in the final two AFL All-Star Games that took place in 1968 and 1969. He was honored by being named to the All-Time American Football League team, and he was inducted into the American Football League Hall of Fame.

Ironically while Philbin played for the Jets, he became the hero of one youngster whose father was a coach on the 1969 team. That coach was Buddy Ryan, who had also been one of his coaches at Buffalo, and Philbin had actually helped open the doors for him to get into the NFL, thanks to his recommendation. And the youngster that so admired Philbin turned out to be future Jets coach Rex Ryan.

Philbin played his 10th and final season in the NFL with the Philadelphia Eagles before finishing his playing career by playing with the New York Stars of the World Football League.

60 Winston Hill

Winston Hill got a quick education about pro football in his early days of camp with the Baltimore Colts in 1963 after getting drafted in the 11th round of the NFL Draft.

Lining up at tackle against veteran defensive end Ordell Braase, Hill learned that even though he might have had the size for the NFL at 6'4" and 270 pounds and the accolades—he earned All-American honors at Southern University—playing offensive and defensive line in college had not properly equipped him. He lacked the techniques and know-how to succeed at that point. Those deficiencies were noted by his coaches, which led to his being asked to turn in his playbook.

Johnny Sample

Johnny Sample came to the Jets as a well-traveled NFL player prior to the 1966 season, but he still had the physical talents and the football knowledge to bolster the Jets' defensive backfield. That knowledge would at times come in how to skirt the rules to gain a competitive advantage.

Sample played for the Baltimore Colts from 1958 to 1960, the Pittsburgh Steelers from 1961 to 1962, and the Washington Redskins from 1963 to 1965.

Among Sample's accomplishments during his 11-year career was the fact that he played for the Colts when they won the 1958 NFL Championship Game against the New York Giants in what is regarded as one of the best games in NFL history, and then he played for the Jets in Super Bowl III in what is generally regarded as the biggest upset in professional football history. He is the only player in professional football history to have won an NFL and AFL championship and a Super Bowl.

Memorable to Jets fans were several of Sample's battles with the top receivers in the league, most notably with Fred Bilitnikoff of the Oakland Raiders during big games such as the AFL Championship Game at the end of the 1968 season. Sample had a big interception in Super Bowl III in which the Jets' defense shut down a high-powered Baltimore attack.

His interception came at the Jets' 2, and in the aftermath of the interception, Sample's reaction came in typical Sample fashion—which would prove to be a precursor for the trash-talking that would later prevail in the NFL.

Clutching the football after intercepting Earl Morrall's pass, Sample bumped the football against the helmet of Baltimore receiver Willie Richardson, who had been Morrall's target on the play. Sample then asked the Baltimore receiver, "This what you're looking for?"

For Sample, the victory in Super Bowl III brought him extra satisfaction because it came against his former team.

Super Bowl III proved to be Sample's final game.

He finished his career with 41 interceptions, of which he returned four for touchdowns.

Following his career, Sample wrote an autobiography that chronicled his playing days and the way many felt he played, appropriately titled *Confessions of a Dirty Ballplayer*.

Following his career, Sample became an accomplished tennis official, who would officiate at big matches at Wimbledon, the U.S. Open, the Australian Open, and the French Open. He died in April 2005.

"[Braase] was the guy who got me cut from Baltimore," said Hill in Mark Kriegel's *Namath*. "I couldn't block him in practice."

Shortly thereafter, Hill changed leagues and signed as a free agent with the Jets, thereby beginning one of the longest consecutive-start streaks in pro football history at 174 games, a streak Sherman Plunkett and Chuck Knox must be given partial credit for enabling.

Plunkett served as a force on the offensive line, and Knox was a Jets assistant from 1963 to 1966. They helped instill in Hill the necessary confidence that would allow him to fulfill his potential and become the left tackle on the offensive line, meaning he would become the man to cover quarterback Joe Namath's blind side.

"I had already been released from Baltimore," said Hill in *Namath*. "I was an offensive tackle trying to take Sherman's job, and it didn't faze him. He would spend time with me after practice. I remember once, I had a lousy day and I was the first one off the field. And Sherman Plunkett called me back and embarrassed me in front of everybody and said, 'Get back there. You know you didn't do anything all day.' We started step by step, making corrections."

Knox also passed on a new blocking technique to Hill and his other offensive linemen. At the time, linemen were not allowed to use their hands to grab defensive linemen as they are today. But Knox had his linemen use their arms by pushing out while leaving their hands open. The technique became an acceptable interpretation of the rule.

Hill would find great success pounding defensive lines to create openings for the likes of Matt Snell, Emerson Boozer, and John Riggins to run through. In addition, he would successfully protect Namath. He made the AFL All-Stars in 1964, 1967, 1968, and 1969. After the merger, he became a Pro Bowl selection in 1970, 1971, 1972, and 1973. Despite all of his success, Hill also had a part in one of the more infamous plays for the Jets in the 1960s.

The Jets were playing the Raiders, who had Ben Davidson playing right defensive end. Davidson personified the Raiders image from his handlebar moustache to the way he liked to play football, always pushing the late hits right at the whistle. Davidson housed all of this energy in a 6'8", 275-pound frame.

Add Davidson's natural inclination to the prevailing wisdom in the AFL that to take out Namath meant taking out the Jets, and you had a recipe for disaster.

Early in the fourth quarter of a Raiders rout in Oakland in 1967, Hill tried to block Davidson and even thought he'd held him off for an adequate amount of time for Namath to safely get off his pass and avoid Davidson. Unfortunately for Hill and Namath, Davidson seemed to have no rules. Namath rolled out of the pocket toward the right sideline and got off a pass that fell incomplete. A second or two then followed before Davidson lowered the boom on Namath, leaving the Jets star fallen on the field without his helmet; later Namath would be diagnosed with a broken cheek from the blow.

Hill would have his most satisfying moment as a professional during Super Bowl III when he tore into his old nemesis, Braase, to open holes for Snell, who gained 121 yards in the Jets' 16–7 win.

Hill played his final season for the Jets in 1976 before finishing his career in 1977 while playing for the Los Angeles Rams.

61 Emerson Boozer

Nobody saw the coming force that Emerson Boozer would bring to the Jets in 1966, not even the Jets.

Boozer went to the University of Maryland Eastern Shore, where his play drew modest interest from the Jets, who drafted him in the sixth round of the 1966 AFL Draft (46th overall selection) and by the Pittsburgh Steelers, who drafted him in the seventh round (98th overall) of the 1966 NFL Draft.

Boozer opted to join the Jets, and during his rookie season he initially split time at fullback with Bill Mathis, while Matt Snell continued to hold a lock on the starting halfback position.

He carried the ball 97 times in 1966 for 455 yards, which was good for 4.7 yards per carry and five touchdowns. Boozer displayed a high motor during his rookie season, whether he was running the football or blocking. By the start of the 1967 season, he earned the right to become the starting fullback.

When Snell got injured in 1967, Boozer became the featured back in the Jets' offense, and he blossomed while showing an ability to break tackles to get into the open field, where he could outrun most defenders. Halfway through his second season, Boozer already had scored 10 touchdowns and appeared to be on the cusp of becoming professional football's next great running back when he incurred a severe knee injury in a game against the Kansas City Chiefs on November 5.

Boozer's 10 touchdowns still led the AFL that season, but the injury changed what Boozer could do on the field.

The consummate professional, Boozer evaluated what his 5'11", 195-pound frame could still do, and he went with it. Since

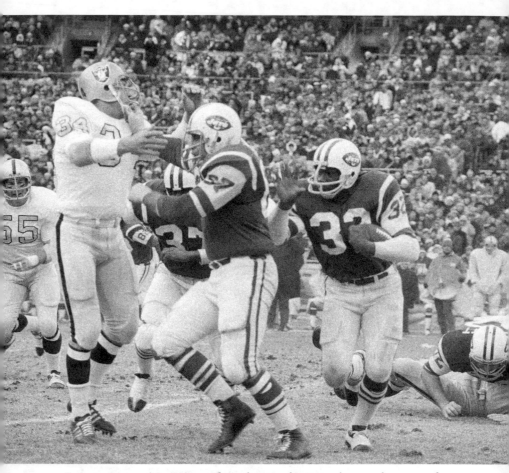

Emerson Boozer (No. 32) goes for a three-yard gain in the second quarter of a game against the Raiders at Shea Stadium on December 6, 1970.

the knee injury altered his speed, he evolved into a short-yardage bulldozer, and he had a talent for catching the ball out of the back-field, which played well in the Jets' passing offense. Above all else, Boozer continued to be a devastating blocker, particularly in pass-blocking situations, which was critical due to the overall offensive mantra of the team that was to protect quarterback Joe Namath at all costs.

Boozer's blocking work could be seen in the results that Snell had rushing the football and Namath had passing the football. Never was that work more evident than during Super Bowl III, when the Jets defeated the Colts 16–7.

Boozer had begun thinking about what the Jets might do in the Super Bowl if given the chance while attending the first NFL-AFL Championship Game between the Green Bay Packers and Kansas City Chiefs in 1967.

"I sat in the stands for Super Bowl I out in L.A., and that game was not a blowout," Boozer told Newsvine.com. "I also sat in the stands for Super Bowl II [Packers-Raiders]. Going into that third year, I thought, *Well, I've seen both games and seen both teams from the AFL play okay but then let it slip away.* I knew we were very capable of beating anybody and that we just had to perform."

Boozer remembered that the game was not "a ho-hum game people would forget."

"It spoke volumes for the AFL," Boozer told Newsvine.com. "We knew that was our last shot at it with the leagues merging [and the AFL and NFL becoming the AFC and NFC]. We knew that would be it. We wanted to be the first club to beat the big boys."

Boozer again became the Jets' featured back in 1973 when he gained 831 yards on 182 carries, which equated to a 4.6-yards-per-carry average. But the next year he had to move to the side for the arrival of John Riggins, the hard-nosed future Hall of Famer from Kansas.

Of note, Boozer's pass-catching ability allowed him to haul in the winning touchdown on a five-yard pass from Namath to give the Jets a 26–20 win over their crosstown rival New York Giants in the NFL's first regular-season sudden-death game on November 10, 1974.

Boozer retired after the 1975 season having spent his entire career with the Jets.

62 Leon Hess

Leon Hess' legacy is tied to the fact that he founded the Hess Corporation, but he is remembered by the sporting public as the man who owned the Jets.

In 1963 Hess became part of a four-man consortium that bought the New York Titans, each of them putting in $250,000 as their share. By 1984 he had bought out all of his partners to become sole owner of the Jets.

A self-made millionaire, Hess parlayed a job driving a heating oil truck during the Depression into ownership of Ameranda Hess Corporation, which he acquired in 1969 after an ownership battle with Phillips Petroleum.

Hess was perceived as a good owner by the public, given the fact that he always fought to improve the team, on and off the field.

Hess and his original partners in the team were responsible for the team becoming the New York Jets and their change of team colors from blue and gold to green and white—it was not coincidental that they were the same colors as those of his Hess gas stations. In addition, the group moved the team from the Polo Grounds to Shea Stadium. While the Jets were at Shea sharing the stadium with the New York Mets, Hess waged a never-ending battle with the city of New York to improve the team's lot.

The Mets had the sweet part of the deal, receiving all parking revenues from Jets games and a portion of the concessions too. He even fought to have the restrooms at Shea improved, as bathroom conditions had been a lifelong pet peeve that also extended to the conditions of the restrooms at his gas stations. Few of his demands were ever met, which eventually led to the team moving to the

Bill Parcells (left) and Jets owner Leon Hess pose with a Jets helmet at the Jets training camp in Hempstead, New York, on February 11, 1997, after Parcells was named the Jets' new head coach.

Meadowlands in East Rutherford, New Jersey, in 1984 to share Giants Stadium with the New York Giants.

Hess did not interfere with football operations as some owners do, allowing the team's football experts to make draft choices and such. And he was not one to become a nuisance by showing up at Jets practices, though he could always be seen at Jets games, normally in the company of Thomas Kean, the governor of New Jersey from 1982 to 1990. He passionately followed the team and rode a wave of emotions that depended on the team's fortunes. If the team lost, he took it hard.

While he rarely interfered with football operations, he did step into the fray in 1995 after the team went 6–10 in 1994, Pete Carroll's first season as head coach. Hess announced that he had fired Carroll and hired Rich Kotite and told reporters at a press conference, "I'm 80 years old. I want results now." Not only was the announcement a shocker, but the fact that he made a public appearance might have been even more shocking. Unlike many owners, who enjoyed a high profile, Hess shied away from interviews throughout his life.

He stepped down as chairman and chief executive officer in 1995, but he continued to serve as the Jets owner and was heavily involved in bringing aboard Bill Parcells in 1997 as the Jets coach after the team had gone 1–15 under Kotite in 1996.

Though Hess did not attend practices, he did hold a tradition of going to the Jets' practice field on Thanksgiving morning accompanied by his family—a visit during which photographs being taken was strictly forbidden. On his last such visit in 1998, he reiterated his dream of seeing the Jets again win the Super Bowl. He would never realize that dream, as he died on May 7, 1999.

63 Dennis Byrd

After four seasons playing for the Jets, Dennis Byrd experienced a profound change in his life when the nightmare every football player fears became a reality for the defensive end/defensive tackle.

The Jets selected Byrd out of the University of Tulsa in the second round of the 1989 NFL Draft, making the 6'5", 270-pound native of Oklahoma City, Oklahoma, the 42nd pick of the draft.

And he played well for the Jets, recording 27 sacks during his first three seasons in the NFL. Then tragedy struck.

On November 29, 1992, the 3–9 Jets hosted the Kansas City Chiefs at the Meadowlands.

Early in the third quarter, Byrd saw Dave Krieg preparing to pass, so he did what any defensive lineman would have done, he pinned his ears back and charged toward the Chiefs quarterback. Once he got close, he lunged for Krieg, who deftly sidestepped the rush. Byrd's head then slammed into teammate Scott Mersereau, who had been rushing from the other side. In doing so, Byrd shattered the C-5 vertebra—one of the 33 bones that make up the spine—and he fell limp to the turf.

"The hit was deafening," Byrd told *Science World*. "I remember the feeling of slowly falling to the ground.... I tried to take my helmet off, to unsnap the snaps with my hand, and it...it just wouldn't work right ... At that point, I began to realize that there wasn't any feeling."

Only days earlier, many of the Jets players had been watching the Detroit Lions play on Thanksgiving Day and saw Mike Utley serving as the Lions' honorary captain from a wheelchair due to an injury he had suffered while playing for the Lions that had left him without the use of his legs.

No doubt that picture materialized in many of the Jets players' heads as doctors tended to their fallen teammate at approximately the 18 at the eastern end of the stadium.

Mersereau, who had taken the blow in his chest, ran to the sideline after the play, unaware that Byrd remained on the field without moving.

"I had no knowledge of what was going on initially, because I was gasping for air," Mersereau told the *New York Times*. "It wasn't until later when I came off on the sidelines, that I saw them take him away."

Doctors and trainers tended to Byrd for over seven minutes as the normally raucous stadium fell silent. He managed to move his left arm but could not move his legs.

"Am I going to be paralyzed? Am I going to be paralyzed?" Byrd asked doctors and trainers over and over while being strapped onto a spine board.

Amazingly, Byrd managed to walk on crutches just 10 weeks later at a press conference at Mount Sinai Hospital in New York. A lot of things had gone right to that point, which had enabled Byrd to defy great odds. Included on the list of things that had gone right was his treatment by professionals who knew what needed to be done to someone in Byrd's predicament—including injections and surgeries—which were steps that helped minimize the damage.

Physical therapy, faith, and a lot of luck took Byrd the rest of the way.

On September 5, 1993, at the Jets' home opener, Byrd walked to midfield as an honorary captain for the coin toss, at which time he was presented with a trophy for the Most Inspirational Player Award by Jets president Steve Gutman. The trophy would come to be known as the Dennis Byrd Award.

Though Byrd's No. 90 has never been officially retired, no Jets player has worn the number since.

64 The Signing of George Sauer Jr.

On New Year's Day 1965, the Jets watched with great interest when the University of Alabama met the University of Texas in the Orange Bowl.

Primarily, the Jets hoped that Alabama quarterback Joe Namath could get through the game without injury, as they had made him the top player selected in the American Football League Draft. To a lesser degree, they wanted to observe a wide receiver for the Longhorns, George Sauer Jr., whom they had also drafted. Unlike Namath, Sauer had not been drafted by an NFL team.

Early in the second quarter with Texas leading 7–0, Sauer hauled in a 69-yard touchdown to expand the Longhorns' lead. Namath brought the Crimson Tide back with a fury, connecting on one pass after the next to earn Orange Bowl MVP honors, but Alabama lost the game 21–17.

While the Jets could have cared less about the game's outcome, they did share a group smile about the possibility of having Namath throwing passes to Sauer at Shea Stadium, each of the pair wearing a Jets uniforms.

Signing Namath came down to a bidding war against the NFL's St. Louis Cardinals. Signing Sauer would prove to be a little more complicated.

Sauer was the son of Jets player personnel director George Sauer Sr., and he wasn't your typical college football jock. Initially he had been a premed student at Texas. After a couple of years at Texas, he expressed to his father his frustrations about being able to make the necessary grades for being a premed student and playing football. At that point he considered giving up the game. His father advised him to take a few days to mull over his decision, which he did. He decided that he liked football too much to quit the sport, so he changed his major to mathematics and remained on the Longhorns team.

In the 1960s, college football did not allow freshmen to be eligible, which left players with three years of eligibility. Sauer had entered Texas in 1961 but did not make the varsity squad as a sophomore, which made him a red-shirt junior during the 1964 season and translated to one more year of eligibility for the Longhorns in the fall of 1965. Only, Sauer decided he wanted to skip his senior season of eligibility to sign a contract to play for the Jets.

A firestorm followed in which Texas coach Darrell Royal went on the warpath against the Jets. Royal told reporters he would refuse consent to Sauer for such a move, which was a hollow threat, considering Sauer did not need his coach's consent to sign a contract.

Self-serving debates about the well-being of the student athlete followed.

Royal equated the practice of the pros talking a player into forsaking his degree to play for money "like talking against motherhood."

AFL commissioner Joe Foss weighed in, going off on Royal by talking about the wrongs of colleges pressuring players to continue in school only because of their athletic ability. Foss summarized by noting, "A man should not be denied the right to work."

Sauer Sr. told the *New York Times*, "Royal is real upset about the whole thing—to the point where he's losing his common sense."

Sauer signed with the Jets on July 12, 1965, much to the chagrin of Royal. The Texas coach offered Sauer good luck. He also made it clear that the Jets would no longer be welcome at Texas and that other teams would be banned in the future if they signed any Texas football players with remaining eligibility.

65 George Sauer Jr.

When George Sauer Jr. came to the Jets in 1965, chemistry between Sauer and Namath became evident from the beginning. During camp prior to both of their rookie seasons, the Jets' rookies were dispatched to play a game against the Boston Patriots' rookies. Namath managed nine completions, five of which Sauer caught. The Jets' future king fell in love with the precise manner in which Sauer ran his routes, a trait that helped the 6'2", 195-pound receiver overcome any speed deficiencies.

Sauer went on to catch 25 passes for 301 yards and two touchdowns during the 1965 season, a season that proved to be a precursor for a grand Jets passing game. By 1967 that aerial attack was in full bloom as Maynard led the AFL with 1,434 receiving yards, which translated to over 20 yards per catch, and Sauer led the league with 75 catches, good for 1,189 yards and six touchdowns. And the Jets' offense thrived as the passing game opened up a solid ground game for big gains.

Namath and Sauer really clicked on the football field. Often they could be seen after practice with Sauer running route after route and Namath finding him with his passes, a practice that enabled the pair to find the precision they would show on Sundays.

"We would invent patterns," said Sauer in Mark Kriegel's *Namath*.

The extra work continued to pay off in 1968 when Sauer caught 66 passes for 1,141 yards and three touchdowns as the Jets marched through the AFL to earn a spot in the Super Bowl against the imposing Baltimore Colts, who had dispatched of the Cleveland Browns 34–0 in the NFL Championship Game. Watching the films from the Colts' lop-sided win gave Sauer a critical insight into the game he would be playing against Baltimore defensive back Lenny Lyles. Right there in front of Sauer the projector showed Cleveland receiver Paul Warfield burning Lyles on a post-corner route. Sauer watched those films and saw the potential for a big day in the big game.

Early in Super Bowl III, Namath overthrew Maynard on a deep pass that covered some 55 yards in the air. Unknown to the Colts, Maynard had been nursing a sore hamstring, which threw off the timing between the pair ever so slightly. The Colts felt like they had dodged a bullet, as Maynard had been open. Had the pass been completed, it would have been a sure touchdown. So they overcompensated on defense to prevent Maynard from burning them again. By doing so, the Colts opened the door for the Jets' running game and for the precise patterns run by Sauer, who suddenly faced only Lyles on the weak side of the field.

Sauer caught passes of four and 11 yards on the Jets' second-quarter drive that culminated with Matt Snell's four-yard touchdown run that gave the Jets a 7–0 lead. Sauer would finish the game with eight catches good for 133 yards as the Jets defeated the Colts 16–7.

Sauer played his last season for the Jets in 1970, having caught 309 passes for 4,965 yards and 28 touchdowns during his six-year career. He finished his professional career by playing for the World Football League's New York Stars in 1971.

66 Al Toon

Al Toon had everything a receiver could want and then some.

While at the University of Wisconsin, the 6'4", 205-pound Toon set a Big Ten record in the triple jump, which earned him a spot in the 1984 Olympic trials. But football was Toon's passion, and when he played the game, anybody watching could tell that he combined that passion with marvelous athletic ability.

The Jets selected Toon in the first round of the 1985 NFL Draft, making him the 10th overall selection. He validated his selection in his rookie season when he caught 46 passes for 662 yards and three touchdowns. From that auspicious beginning, Toon seemed to get better every season.

After five seasons, Toon had caught 355 passes, which was more than any receiver had caught in their first five years in NFL history. In 1988 he had his best season when he led the league with 93 receptions for 1,067 yards and five touchdowns.

Unfortunately, some of the traits that made Toon a special player also led to his demise. Among those traits was his fearlessness, always refusing to go down until he could go no longer. Playing in such a manner often left him vulnerable to big hits by defenders, who finally stopped him from gaining additional yardage. During a 1987 exhibition game between the Jets and the Giants, Giants linebackers lowered the boom on Toon, causing what would be the first of many concussions.

Still, Toon led the Jets in receptions for six straight years through 1991 and was voted to the Pro Bowl three times. Typifying Toon's professionalism was his performance on November 6, 1988, when the Jets played the Indianapolis Colts. Toon was sleep-deprived from the time he'd spent at the hospital for the birth of his son Nicholas, but he still managed to haul in 13 passes for 106 yards.

"The biggest problem I have with Al Toon is he tried to do everything too perfectly," Jets receivers coach Chip Myers told the *New York Times*. "You don't ask wide receivers to block ordinarily, but we asked him to block because we were going to get the running game cranked up, and he's one of the best blockers that ever played the game. I mean, he just doesn't miss. Ever. He knew what to do as far as catching the ball and running with it. He's a potential big play on every down, but the funny thing was, he never really believed he could block like he did."

Toon had suffered four concussions by the time Broncos linebacker Michael Brooks hit him on a play during a 27–16 loss at Denver in 1992. Toon did not play in the aftermath of the blow that caused the fifth concussion of his career. Toon began to experience loss of memory and trouble performing day-to-day activities, which prompted many tests and doctor visits. All of which pointed to the obvious conclusion that he needed to retire to avoid serious consequences.

"You go to a doctor and get an opinion, and you go to more than one doctor and get more than one opinion," said Toon, upon retiring on November 27, 1992. "You get multiple opinions. If all are the same, or concur with the decision, you have to rely on it."

At the time of Toon's retirement, he held team records for the most catches in a season with 93 and for having the most consecutive games with a reception at 101. His 517 catches ranked second behind Don Maynard's 627, and he ranked third in club history in receiving yardage with 6,605 behind Maynard (11,732) and Wesley Walker (6,306).

Toon had a great but bittersweet career with the Jets. Without the concussions, he might have ranked among the best receivers in professional football history.

67 Boomer Esiason

By the time Julius "Boomer" Esiason arrived on the Jets in 1993, his body of work as an NFL quarterback had been completed while playing quarterback for the Cincinnati Bengals.

But the 6'5", 224-pound southpaw from West Islip, New York, still had enough physical skills remaining to complement his immense football IQ to be effective for the Jets. And he became a fan favorite from the minute he arrived at the Meadowlands.

Esiason had ties to the area dating back to Timber Point Elementary and East Islip High School on Long Island, New York. People remembered the three-sport athlete who left the area in 1979 to begin a football career at the University of Maryland.

Playing for Bobby Ross, Esiason set plenty of records for the Terrapin football program before the Bengals drafted him in the second round of the 1984 NFL Draft, making him the 38th selection. Ironically, despite being a low selection relative to where he was projected to go, Esiason was the first quarterback taken in the draft.

He became one of the most prolific quarterbacks in the league, running the high-powered Bengals offense. Particularly effective at running the play-action offense, Esiason earned MVP honors when he reached the summit of his nine-year stint in Cincinnati by leading the Bengals to Super Bowl XXIII, where they faced the San Francisco 49ers, who were led by future Hall of Fame quarterback Joe Montana.

The Bengals led 16–13 and appeared to have the game won when Montana led the 49ers on a 92-yard drive that culminated with a touchdown pass to John Taylor with 34 seconds left on the clock. The Bengals lost 20–16.

Esiason joined the Jets in 1993 when they traded a third-round pick in the 1993 NFL Draft to the Bengals to acquire him. In his first season with the team, his presence seemed to spark some magic as he completed 60.9 percent of his passes, but the team finished 8–8 after losing four of its final five games.

Though Esiason remained popular with the fans, his tenure with the Jets did not end well, which was due in large part to the situation the Jets put him in during his final two seasons with the team, failing to give him much of a cast of players around him.

Esiason suffered a bad concussion in that final season with the team in 1995, and they finished a dismal 3–13. Still, he expressed a desire to return to the Jets for a fourth season in 1996. But that did not happen, as the Jets released him.

During his three years with the team, Esiason started 42 games and played in 43. Despite completing 764 of 1,302 passes—good for 58.7 percent and 8,478 yards—the Jets went 15–27 in games Esiason started.

Prior to the 1996 season, he signed as a free agent with the Arizona Cardinals. He finished off his 14-year career with a return stop with the Bengals in 1997 and retired after that season. Befitting Esiason's excellence was his final play in the NFL that saw him throw a 70-yard touchdown pass to receiver Darnay Scott for the winning touchdown in a 16–14 Bengals win over the Baltimore Ravens.

During his career, Esiason made the Pro Bowl four times and earned first-team All-Pro honors one season. To Jets fans, he remained the local boy done good.

68 Wayne Chrebet

Easily one of the all-time fan favorites for the Jets, Wayne Chrebet signed with the team as a non-drafted free agent out of Hofstra in 1995, and by the time he retired after the 2005 season, he had earned the much-respected nickname of "Mr. Third Down."

"He inspired me every day," running back Curtis Martin told the Associated Press. "I loved the way he played and how he never backed down from anything. He was an incredible teammate. He was a warrior, and I always felt you'd have to kill him to get the upper hand on him. If every player in the NFL had as much heart and desire as he had, football would be illegal."

Chrebet hailed from Garfield, New Jersey, where he was an all-county and all-area football selection in addition to earning letters in basketball and baseball at Garfield High School.

From there he went to Hofstra, where he majored in criminal justice and specialized in his passion, football, finishing second on Hofstra's all-time receptions and receiving-yardage lists.

When Chrebet showed up at the Jets' camp, the odds of the 5'10", 188-pound receiver making the team were not far greater than Namath's Jets winning Super Bowl III; the odds for him to even get a chance at training camp were somewhat lop-sided as well. Arriving for his first workout with the team, a security guard refused to let him in because he did not look like a player. Once in camp, Chrebet stared down the odds and got to work trying to move up the depth chart and make the team.

Through effort and ability, Chrebet beat the odds and made the team, becoming the first Hofstra player to win an NFL job since John Schmidt had done so in 1964. Chrebet didn't take time to celebrate. He simply did what he did best by getting to work, making 66 catches for 726 yards and four touchdowns in his rookie season. That season would be the beginning of a beautiful marriage between the diminutive receiver and the Jets faithful.

Highlighting his rookie season were the games against the St. Louis Rams, when he caught eight passes and managed to drag a Rams defender on his way to the end zone, and against the Jacksonville Jaguars, when he caught 12 passes for 162 yards, with five of his catches going for first downs. After catching 96 passes in his second season, Chrebet established an NFL record for most receptions by a wide receiver in his first two seasons.

Chrebet wore No. 80, which became a favorite in the stands due as much to his character as his play. He maintained a respectful manner toward teammates, opponents, and fans, which brought a striking contrast to the likes of his teammate Keyshawn Johnson. After leaving the Jets, the flamboyant Johnson noted that any comparisons between Chrebet and himself would be "like comparing a flashlight to a star."

Chrebet's career came to a close on November 6, 2005, when he suffered the fifth concussion of his career. Fittingly, Chrebet hung on to the ball on the third-down play to earn the Jets a first down. Of his 580 career receptions, 379 were good for first downs. At the time of his retirement, his 580 receptions placed him second on the Jets' all-time receiving list, his 7,365 receiving yards placed him in the team's top five, and he caught 41 touchdowns.

"His story is that of a long shot, a consummate overachiever," team owner Woody Johnson said upon Chrebet's retirement. "Wayne's trajectory of success represents everything that is great about this sport."

69 Vinny Testaverde

Vinny Testaverde arrived in the NFL in 1987 from the University of Miami as the first pick of the Tampa Bay Buccaneers, a struggling franchise that possessed the top pick of the NFL Draft.

At 6'5" and 235 pounds, the strong-armed Testaverde was looked upon to work miracles for the hapless Buccaneers, and the expectations were well founded based on his body of work. While at Miami, he became the Hurricanes' all-time leader in touchdown passes with 48, and he claimed the 1986 Heisman Trophy. Unfortunately for Testaverde, he had talented players to complement him at Miami, which he did not while in Tampa, where the job proved to be too much for the as-yet-to-ripen quarterback.

When things go bad for an NFL team, the quarterback usually gets the blame. Testaverde didn't exactly play well for the Bucs, but he certainly didn't deserve the snarky barbs he received, some of

Vinny Testaverde throws under pressure from Atlanta Falcons defensive end Lester Archambeau in first-quarter action on October 25, 1998.

which mocked the fact that he was color blind. A memorable local billboard showed Testaverde positioned in front of a blue background. The sign read, "Vinny thinks this is orange!"

Not until later in his career would Testaverde come into his own.

By the time Testaverde joined the Jets in 1998, he had matured into a solid—and well preserved—NFL quarterback.

All of the misfortune Testaverde experienced earlier in his career seemed to work in his direction the older he got in the league. After spending six seasons with the Bucs, Testaverde played three with the Browns and two with the Ravens in advance of the Brooklyn native returning home and putting on the green and white in Bill Parcells' second season coaching the team.

Fun Over 40

December 26, 2005, marked the end of an era. *Monday Night Football* telecast its final game on ABC, the network that invented the concept of showing NFL games to a prime-time audience; *Monday Night Football* moved to ESPN the following season.

The final game ABC showed: the Jets playing the New England Patriots.

Not only did the game bring a historic moment in broadcast history, it also brought history in the form of quarterback combatants Vinny Testaverde and Doug Flutie. The former Heisman Trophy winners would mark the game with an interesting and odd occurrence.

Both were at the end of their respective NFL careers at the time, and both were backups entering the game.

Flutie backed up Tom Brady for the Patriots, while Testaverde played second fiddle to Brooks Bollinger on the Jets.

With just over three minutes to play in the game, the 42-year-old Testaverde replaced Bollinger and a minute later connected with Laveranues Coles on a 27-yard touchdown to make him the first player in NFL history to throw a touchdown pass in 19 straight seasons. Down on the turf at the Meadowlands there was something poetic about the moment coming on *Monday Night Football* since one of Testaverde's most memorable moments had occurred in an *MNF* game telecast on October 23, 2000, when he threw four touchdowns in the fourth quarter to complete one of the biggest comebacks in NFL history.

On this night, Testaverde finished with three completions in seven passes for 63 yards.

Meanwhile, the 43-year-old Flutie entered the game from the other sideline to complete the only pass he threw, which proved to be the final pass of his career.

Regardless of what either quarterback did in the game, the fact that Testaverde and Flutie in fact played in that game brought a historic NFL moment to pass since it was the first time in NFL history that two quarterbacks over the age of 40 competed in a regular-season game against each other.

Testaverde would not play during the 2006 season before returning in 2007 to play his final season in the NFL with the Carolina Panthers.

The Jets became the beneficiaries of what would be Testaverde's best NFL season in his first year with the team when he threw 29 touchdowns—with just seven interceptions—while serving as the leader for a squad that won the AFC East with a record of 12–4.

Once in the playoffs, Testaverde led the team to a 34–24 win over the Jacksonville Jaguars in a contest that saw him complete 24 of the 36 passes he threw, including a touchdown to Keyshawn Johnson. The team ran out of steam the following week at Denver, where the Broncos, who went on to win the Super Bowl, shut down the Jets' rushing attack, allowing just 14 yards on the ground. The Jets were forced to go to the air, and Testaverde completed 31 of his 56 throws for 356 yards, but the Jets lost 23–10.

While the Jets had not finished the job in 1998, that season fueled high expectations for 1999, which proved to be a disappointing season that saw the Jets regress to 8–8 due largely to Testaverde tearing a tendon in his knee and missing most of the season.

Parcells left after 1999, but Testaverde remained with the Jets for three more seasons. The highlight of his final three seasons came in 2000 when he led a memorable comeback against the Miami Dolphins with a *Monday Night Football* audience watching while the Jets erased a 31–7 fourth-quarter lead to take a 40–37 win. Testaverde threw five touchdown passes in that game, which came to be known as "the Monday Night Miracle."

Testaverde left the Jets in 2004 to play for the Dallas Cowboys, then returned to the team in 2005 in a backup role. He played his final season in 2007 for the Carolina Panthers, retiring at the age of 44.

At the time of his retirement, Testaverde held several NFL records, including throwing touchdown passes to 70 different players.

70 Aaron Glenn's Magic

Nothing is more demoralizing to the opposing team than having the unexpected happen, resulting in the other team scoring a touchdown.

Aaron Glenn became the master of deflating the opposition with two of the most logic-defying plays in Jets history.

The first of these occurred when the Jets played the Dolphins on September 15, 1996.

Dan Marino was celebrating his 35th birthday, and midway through the second quarter Glenn put an early damper on the Dolphins quarterback's party when he stepped in front of one of his passes at the goal line and then returned the interception 100 yards for a touchdown, thereby silencing the crowd at Joe Robbie Stadium.

Unfortunately for the Jets, despite building a 14–0 lead, Marino eventually got things going—throwing three touchdown passes—and the Jets took a 36–27 loss.

"One play, one player like Aaron Glenn cannot carry the whole team," Jets receiver Webster Slaughter said after the game. "He tried to get us started. A lot of other people never reached his level. It all boils down to consistency."

Just over two years later on November 15, 1998, lightning struck again when the 6–3 Jets traveled to Indianapolis to play the 1–8 Colts. The Jets led 16–10 with time running out in the first half when Colts quarterback Peyton Manning ran out of bounds trying to stop the clock so they could try a field goal. Time appeared to have run out on the play, thereby ending the first half. But the officials ended up putting one second back on the clock, which allowed the Colts to try a 63-yard field goal.

Sixty-three yards stood as the record for the longest field goal in NFL history, so the idea that Colts kicker Mike Vanderjagt could make such a kick might have seemed preposterous. Then again, he stood 6'5" and weighed 210 pounds with kicking distance in his leg reflecting that size. So what did the Colts have to lose? No matter what Vanderjagt did, the play would be the final one of the first half, and if the magic happened, the Jets' lead would be reduced to 16–13.

Vanderjagt did not make the kick, but the ball came down into Glenn's waiting arms. What happened next appeared to be a combination of athletic skill and confusion as Glenn returned the ball out of the end zone. The run seemed to take advantage of the hulking personnel the Colts had on the field—who were on the field to block for a field goal rather than being used to cover a kick—and there seemed to be a general lack of awareness of what the rule was for returning kicks.

The 5'9", 185-pound jitterbug began his way up the field, weaving back and forth until finally making his way toward the left sideline. From there he sprinted the rest of the way to the end zone. All told, approximately 17 seconds had passed as Glenn covered 104 yards on the return, which broke Al Nelson's record with the Philadelphia Eagles, when he had returned a field goal 101 yards in 1971. The Jets took a 23–10 lead into the intermission, no doubt full of confidence they were on their way to victory.

Unfortunately for the Jets, long returns of any kind by Glenn seemed to jinx the team rather than inspire them. The Jets did not score a point in the second half, while Manning threw touchdowns to Marvin Harrison and Marcus Pollard to take a 24–23 win.

Glenn spent eight seasons with the Jets before heading to the Houston Texans in 2002. Jets fans will always remember him for being a talented cornerback as well as the guy who made two electrifying plays.

71 Herman Edwards

Herman Edwards had the Jets fans at "hello" when the team hired him to succeed Al Groh.

Anybody who could cause the anguish for the New York Giants that Edwards had during his playing days was welcome as far as the forces of green and white were concerned.

Edwards spent the first nine of his 10 NFL seasons playing defensive back for the Philadelphia Eagles from 1977 through 1986, making 135 consecutive regular-season starts and 33 career interceptions. He spent his final season in the league with the Los Angeles Rams and Atlanta Falcons in 1986 and then retired.

For all of his excellence as a player, Edwards is remembered most—and beloved by Jets fans—for a play that took place in a game between the Eagles and the Giants on November 19, 1978. The Giants held a 17–12 lead, the Eagles had no timeouts left, and little time remained. The logical call would have been for Giants quarterback Joe Pisarcik to take a knee after the center snapped him the football. By doing so, the clock would have run out, and the Eagles would have left the Meadowlands losers that day. Inexplicably, Pisarcik tried to hand the ball off to Larry Csonka, and the exchange did not go smoothly. The ball fell to the ground, Edwards charged in, scooped up the football, and returned it 26 yards for a touchdown that gave the Eagles a 19–17 win in what New Yorkers would come to call "the Fumble."

Thus, when Edwards took over as the Jets' coach, the fans of the team already had something they liked a great deal about their new coach.

Even though Edwards had not been a head coach or even a coordinator when he arrived, he had the kind of pedigree that

Snowball, Anyone?

"Don't get mad, get even," is the way Jets defensive end Shaun Ellis looked at the situation.

On December 21, 2008, the Jets had just dropped a 13–3 game to the Seahawks in Seattle when they walked toward the locker room at Qwest Field. While the Jets walked, they were pelted with snowballs by the fans. Ellis decided he had enough and opted to take matters into his own hands by reaching into the snow and constructing his own ammunition in the form of an oversized snowball. Once armed with the snowball that took two hands to carry, he tossed it into the stands, where it hit a few fans. He did not stop to watch the damage, he just continued toward the locker room. Nobody was hurt by Ellis' snowball, and he maintained he had no malice in his actions.

"It was kind of like a little battlefield out there, so to speak," Ellis said. "I mean, it was just all in fun, going to the locker room."

A fan caught Ellis' action on film and posted it on YouTube in the form of a 53-second clip that got approximately 340,000 viewers the first day.

Typical of the NFL, which is the acronym for "No Fun League," they fined Ellis $10,000 for his actions.

NFL players are made aware before every season that they may not make contact with the fans in any sort of manner that might cause crowd-control issues or risk of injury. In addition, players are not to confront fans during games. Any issues with fans must be taken care of by security personnel and not the players.

Ellis had been arrested for speeding and marijuana possession a month before the Seattle incident, which did not help his cause.

Seattle coach Mike Holmgren, who was coaching his final home game as the coach of the Seahawks, also got pelted with snowballs, but he understood the situation and managed to have a sense of humor. He noted that the Seahawks had previously played indoors at the Kingdome from 1976 to 1999 and that snow rarely fell on the area, so the temptation to unload with the snowballs was too much for most of the fans to take.

"I know if my grandkids were up there, and there was a snowball sitting right there—and they're good kids, they're not mean kids—it'd be pretty hard for them not to throw it," Holmgren said.

suggested he could continue the winning path Parcells had the Jets on when he left and Al Groh took over for one season in 2000. He had more than paid his dues with stops at San Jose State as a defensive assistant, the Kansas City Chiefs as a defensive backs coach, and with the Tampa Bay Buccaneers as a defensive backs/assistant head coach. He'd also worked as a scout for the Chiefs.

Edwards inherited a talented and experienced team from Groh (which had largely been assembled by Parcells), which helped the Jets reach the playoffs in Edwards' first two seasons with the team. But the Jets lost to the Raiders in the first round of the 2001 playoffs, and the following season they lost to the Raiders again after winning in the first round.

The Jets did not make the playoffs in 2003, but they did in 2004 and again lost, this time to the Pittsburgh Steelers. In 2005 the Jets bottomed out with a 4–12 record in advance of Edwards' bizarre departure from the Jets.

After countless rumors about Edwards going to the Chiefs to replace retiring legend Dick Vermeil, it became evident that the Chiefs truly wanted Edwards to become their head coach. The fact that Edwards had a personal relationship with Chiefs president Carl Peterson added to the Chiefs' desire to bring him aboard. Even though Edwards had two years left on his contract, the Jets and Chiefs reached an arrangement that saw the Chiefs trade a fourth-round selection in the 2006 NFL Draft to the Jets for Edwards.

Edwards finished his tenure with the Jets at 39–41 during the regular season and 2–3 in playoff games. Over the course of his final 20 games with the Jets, the team compiled a 5–15 mark. Once Edwards left for the Chiefs, the Jets replaced him with Eric Mangini.

72 Chad Pennington

Chad Pennington didn't have great size or an overwhelming arm, but nobody could dispute the fact that he was a born leader and a winner.

Pennington had been the underdog throughout his athletic career dating as far back as high school.

After finishing his senior season at Webb School in Knoxville, Tennessee, just three colleges offered him a scholarship, and he opted to head to Marshall University in Huntington, West Virginia. Playing for the Thundering Herd, Pennington proved he belonged by starting his freshman year only to be made to red-shirt his sophomore season. But the move paid off, and by his senior year in 1999, he led Marshall to a 13–0 record and a Mid-American Conference championship, finishing fifth in the voting for the Heisman Trophy.

The Jets drafted Pennington in the first round of the 2000 NFL Draft, making him the 18th player selected that year. And once again he found himself on the sideline waiting for his chance while he watched Vinny Testaverde lead the team during the 2000 and 2001 seasons, which saw Pennington play in a total of three games and complete 12 of the 25 passes he attempted.

Pennington's chance finally came in the fifth game of the 2002 season. Injecting new life into a 1–4 team, he led the Jets to wins in eight of their final 11 games to win the AFC East with a 9–7 record. Along the way, he completed 68.9 percent of his passes (275 of 399) for 3,120 yards and 22 touchdowns. Pennington then engineered a 41–0 win over the Indianapolis Colts in the first round of the playoffs before bowing out of the postseason with a 30–10 loss to the Oakland Raiders.

Pennington suffered a combination fracture and dislocation to his left hand during the 2003 preseason, which stalled the beginning of his season. When he returned to the team after five games, the Jets had only won once. They went on to win just five more games in 2003.

From that season on, Pennington's career with the Jets was dotted with excellence and assorted injuries. From 2000 through 2007, he completed 65.6 percent (1,259 of 1,919) of his passes for 82 touchdowns and 13,738 yards during the regular season. He threw another seven touchdowns in his five postseason starts for the Jets.

Perhaps Pennington's most amazing season for the team came in 2006 when he returned after having his second rotator cuff surgery. Despite dealing with reduced strength on his passes, Pennington started all 16 games and threw for 3,352 yards in a new offense that utilized the short pass. By the end of the season, the Jets had experienced an astounding turnaround from 4–12 in 2005 to 10–6 in 2006 and a berth in the playoffs. Pennington won the Associated Press NFL Comeback Player of the Year Award after the 2006 season.

Every team in the NFL constantly is trying to improve its chances of winning, and the Jets were no different in 2008. They thought they saw an opportunity that might allow them to go all the way by bringing in future Hall of Fame quarterback Brett Favre to run their offense. In order to make room for Favre, the Jets let Pennington go during training camp.

Pennington signed with the Miami Dolphins and led them to an 11–5 season and a spot in the playoffs, while Favre, playing through an injury, was not able to get the Jets to the postseason.

73 Eric Mangini

If you can't beat them, join them, or at least try and be like them. Such was some of the logic used by the Jets when hiring Eric Mangini to be the team's head coach on January 17, 2006.

Bill Belichick's New England Patriots had been having their way with the Jets for years. Everything the NFL coaching savant did worked, from the personnel moves he made to the game-calling he did on Sundays, and the Jets were often left in the wake of Belichick's successes since they were also members of the AFC East.

Mangini had enjoyed a relationship with Belichick for years, which no doubt added to his résumé when applying for the Jets position after Herman Edwards went to the Kansas City Chiefs following the 2005 season. The fact that Magnini had a relationship at all with Belichick served as a testament to his work ethic.

Belichick had been the coach of the Cleveland Browns 12 years earlier when he noticed the team's young ball boy, Mangini, because of how hard he went about his business. That recognition led Mangini toward taking the unconventional path through the Browns' public-relations office to having a job as an assistant with the team. From there he went to the Baltimore Ravens for a season as an offensive assistant. In 1996 he rejoined his mentor as a defensive assistant with the Jets after Belichick became the team's defensive coordinator. Subsequently, he followed Belichick to New England when he became the team's head coach in 2000.

While with New England, Mangini coached the defensive backs for five years before he moved into a role as the team's defensive coordinator in 2005.

He became head coach of the Jets at the age of 35, making him the youngest head coach in the league at the time. Mangini brought along with him the confidence of youth and a swagger from having been associated with New England's success, as the Patriots had won three Super Bowls while Mangini was there.

"What I learned in New England about teamwork, discipline, how an organization should be run, how a team should be coached, I wouldn't trade for anything in the world," Mangini told *Sports Illustrated.* "What I learned is that even when you're on top, as we were, it wasn't good enough. You always had to work to stay ahead of the curve."

Mangini looked like the right hire in his first season when the Jets went 10–6 in 2006 after having posted a 4–12 mark in Edwards' last season with the team in 2005. Unfortunately for the Jets, the 2006 season would be the high-water mark of his tenure with the team.

In Mangini's second season, an event occurred that turned out to be the defining moment of his time with the Jets when he filed a complaint with NFL officials about the Jets' defensive signals being filmed by Belichick's Patriots, an action deemed a rules violation. The incident came to be known as Spygate, and in the aftermath of the scandal, Belichick got fined and suspended. However, Mangini ratting out his mentor did nothing to help the Jets, who went 4–12 in 2007.

Mangini's third season saw the Jets burst out of the gate by winning eight of their first 11 games. But they won just once more that season, which led to Mangini being fired the day after the 2008 season ended.

Less than two weeks later, the Cleveland Browns hired Mangini to be their head coach.

74 2,000 Yards and Weeb's Finale

Long before O.J. Simpson would become infamous for deeds away from the football field, he lived larger than life as the star running back for the Buffalo Bills. While with the Bills he cemented his legacy with a generation of professional football fans through his accomplishments during the 1973 season, which culminated with a game against the Jets on December 16, 1973.

Most of the talk leading up to the game between the Bills and the Jets for the final game of the season focused on the fact that Simpson would enter the game just 61 yards short of breaking Jim Brown's single-season rushing mark of 1,863 set with the Cleveland Browns in 1963.

At 8–5, the Bills also still had a slim chance at making the playoffs if they could defeat the 4–9 Jets at Shea Stadium. The game would also hold significance for Jets fans, as longtime coach Weeb Ewbank had announced that the 1973 season would be his last as the team's head coach.

Given the fact that the Jets had little to gain and the fact that Simpson enjoyed great popularity, the popular sentiment for what people wanted to see was obvious. William N. Wallace of the *New York Times* wrote in advance of the game, "So popular and spectacular is Simpson, and so meaningless is Sunday's game at Shea Stadium against the Buffalo Bills, that if the Jet defenders hold Simpson down it will be as if they shot Santa Claus."

America embraced Simpson like they did popular characters on family sitcoms, and he never disappointed, always saying the right things. Heading into the game, he deflected attention toward him to his offensive line by saying, "We have the cockiest offensive line in football. They think they can do anything for me. Reggie [McKenzie] keeps saying I'm going to get 2,000 yards. They keep cheering me on."

And about the Jets, he said, "They've given me trouble in the past." Meaning they managed to hold him to just under 123 yards when the two teams met on September 30, 1973.

Meanwhile, a loss by the Jets would give the team a 4–10 mark, thereby matching the worst record in team history that had been accomplished by the 1970 squad. No matter the outcome, Ewbank would be leaving the game with a winning record, as he took a 130–128–7 mark into the final game of his coaching career.

Typical of Jets seasons in those days, rumors also circulated that Joe Namath might also be playing his final game due to the degenerating condition of his surgically repaired knees, but Jets fans were used to the Namath rumor that seemed to greet the end of each and every season.

Shea Stadium had a blanket of snow covering the turf, which did little to slow down Simpson as he surpassed Brown's record on the Bills' second possession of the game when he ran for six yards through a hole opened by right guard Joe DeLamielleure at the expense of Jets defensive lineman Mark Lomas. Timeout was called, affording officials the opportunity to award Simpson the football after his historic carry. He carried the ball to the sideline, where his teammates mobbed him. Given the fact that the first quarter wasn't even complete, the Bills began to focus on a bigger mark. Simpson continued to chew up the Jets' defense, which inspired the Bills to focus on helping Simpson reach what seemed to be an unattainable mark of 2,000 yards.

Early in the fourth quarter, the Bills rookie quarterback Joe Ferguson reached the huddle and informed his teammates that Simpson needed just 50 more yards to reach 2,000 for the season. With 6:28 remaining, Simpson went off left guard for a gain of seven yards to put the ball at the Jets' 13, which gave him 200 yards on 34 carries for the afternoon, equating to 2,003 yards for the season.

The gracious crowd at Shea Stadium cheered for Simpson while his teammates hoisted him on their shoulders.

Namath finished off the Jets' 1973 season by connecting with Rich Caster on a 16-yard touchdown that made the final score Bills 34, Jets 14.

In the Jets' locker room after the game, an emotional Ewbank accepted a gold watch from his team before the 66-year-old coach told them, "We've had good days here and we've had bad days. You're still great. Come back next year and win 'em all."

Namath, who had developed a special bond with Ewbank over the years, would say he had to fight back tears watching his coach ride off into the sunset.

Evolution of the Jets Uniform

In 1960, when the New York Jets were known as the New York Titans, the team's uniforms looked nothing like what future generations of Jets teams would wear.

The Titans' color scheme was navy blue and gold, and the uniform was drastically understated when compared to the team uniforms that would follow as well as those worn by the rest of the league. In essence, the Titans' uniform brought a University of Michigan sort of flavor to the team, even though they lacked the Wolverines' helmet design. *Plain* would be the best way to describe the original fashion statement made by the Titans, but you wouldn't go so far as to call the uniforms drab.

Here Don Maynard sports the earliest incarnation of the Titans uniforms. There have been myriad permutations between this and today's Jets uniforms.

Merchandisers of today would have choked up a lung after observing the absence of any kind of team identification or symbol on either the jersey or the helmet. The home jersey was navy blue with gold letters, and the helmet was navy blue. The snappiest element of the uniform came on the sides of the gold pants where two thin blue stripes ran the length of the pants leg.

A major overhaul came in the 1963 season when the team colors changed to green and white and the design of the uniforms incorporated stripes and a team logo. Two thin green stripes could be found on either side of a thick stripe on each shoulder of the jersey. Within the large stripe, the player's number could be found; the number was displayed on the front and back of the jersey as well. On either side of the white helmet was the logo of a green plane with *JETS* written inside the plane's shape; a green stripe ran from front to back on the helmet.

In 1965 the logo changed to the shape of a green football with *JETS* written inside of the football. Featured in the background of the logo was an outline of *NY*.

Subtle changes took place in 1968 when the shoulder stripes were altered slightly and a green belt replaced the white belt on the pants.

Radical changes came 10 years later when the logo changed along with the jerseys and the color of the helmets. The middle shoulder stripe was eliminated, moving the numbers that had been on the outside of the upper arms to the top of the shoulder pads. The new logo had *JETS* spelled out in a sleek, modern font, while the helmet color became green.

A thin green or white ring around the jersey collar was added in 1986—depending on whether the team wore its white or green jerseys. The team's white pants also gained a green stripe down the outside of both legs.

Thin black stripes were added to the outsides of the stripes and numbers in 1990. In addition, the team began to wear green pants when they wore their white jerseys.

Tiny *NFL* logos were added to the front of the collar of the jerseys as well as to the left thigh of the pants in 1993. In addition, a patch commemorating the 25th anniversary of the Super Bowl was placed at the front of the jerseys' left shoulders. Contained within that patch for the Jets was recognition of the team's win in Super Bowl III.

A blast from the past hit the Jets' fashion world in 1994, as the team went back to the jersey with the three stripes, and all teams wore a patch commemorating the NFL's 75th anniversary. The logo on the side of the helmet also reverted back to the one introduced in 1965, but the color of the helmet remained green.

The 1998 season saw the Jets continue to reach back to the past by reintroducing the white helmets. A Jets logo was also placed on the jersey in front of the left shoulder.

Facing the beginning of a new century in 2000, the Jets incorporated elements from several uniforms. Among the changes was a return to the green helmet with *JETS* in a modern font.

Today, with the popularity of throwback uniforms, any possible fashion combination can be seen on the Jets' sideline on any given Sunday.

76 Visit the Orange Bowl

Yes, the Orange Bowl met its demise in May 2008 when it was demolished, but even though the structure itself is gone, any Jets fan needs to make the trek to Miami and stand on the site of where the greatest game in the team's history took place on January 12, 1969.

Of course that was the day the Jets defeated the Baltimore Colts 16–7 in Super Bowl III.

Located west of downtown Miami in the Little Havana area of Miami, the Orange Bowl, originally named Burdine Stadium, was renamed the Orange Bowl in 1959 to reflect the name of the college football bowl game hosted at the stadium from 1938 through 1995. The stadium sat in the middle of a sizeable block of real estate bound on the north end by Northwest 6th Street, on the east by Northwest 14th Avenue, on the south by Northwest 3rd Street, and on the west by Northeast 16th Avenue. To get one's bearings, the open end of the Orange Bowl was east.

When Super Bowl III was played, the venue remained one of the Cadillac spots in sports and carried a grandiose prestige attached to the experience of playing there. In the stadium's heyday, there were no retractable-roof stadiums or luxury boxes; the only item of interest took place on the field for the spectators to watch.

The Jets were familiar with the Orange Bowl from playing the Miami Dolphins, who called the Orange Bowl home for 21 seasons before moving to Joe Robbie Stadium, located in Miami Gardens, in 1987. The Orange Bowl also played host to home games for the University of Miami football program, as the Hurricanes began playing there in 1937 and continued doing so through the 2007 season before moving to Joe Robbie. At one point the Hurricanes won 58 consecutive home games from 1985 through 1994 until the streak came to an end against the University of Washington.

The Dolphins also enjoyed a great home-field advantage at the Orange Bowl, particularly against their AFC East rivals. Other than having a perfect Super Bowl record at the Orange Bowl, the Jets had little success there over the years, posting a 4–13–1 mark. Like the U, the Dolphins also put together an extensive home winning streak by winning 31 straight at the Orange Bowl from 1971 to 1975.

Several factors contributed to the home-field advantage for teams calling the Orange Bowl home, among them the acoustics in the west end zone that amplified the noise and, naturally, the South Florida heat, particularly when the field had an AstroTurf surface from 1970 through January 1976. Temperatures on the artificial surface routinely would exceed 110 degrees and literally cook the chances for opposing teams to defeat the Dolphins, whose games were normally played on Sunday afternoons.

On March 3, 2008, demolition of the Orange Bowl began, and the deed was finished on May 14, 2008. A 37,000-seat retractable-roof baseball stadium for the Florida Marlins is being built on the site and is scheduled to open in 2012. Those wanting to get a feel for the historic stadium that once held such prominence in the football world can be treated to artwork that uses the letters that composed *Miami Orange Bowl*.

No nostalgic trip for any Jets fan would be complete without putting on your No. 12 Joe Namath jersey and running toward the location of where the west end zone once sat. Once the vibe hits you, be sure to raise your right hand with your index finger pointing skyward to signify No. 1 as Broadway Joe once did on that memorable January afternoon in 1969.

77 Joe Walton

On January 9, 1983, Joe Walton's best got put on display.

Trailing the Cincinnati Bengals 14–3 in the first round of the playoffs at Riverfront Stadium, the Jets needed something to kick-start the team out of a lethargic start.

Serving as the Jets' offensive coordinator under head coach Walt Michaels, Walton made the bold call: "Fake 38 sweep option pass."

All season long Walton had admired the tight spirals thrown by Freeman McNeil. For whatever reason, the Jets running back just had a knack for throwing the football. Tucking that thought away for a later day, that day came in Cincinnati with the play Walton had installed into the Jets' offense to take advantage of McNeil's arm.

McNeil took the ball from quarterback Richard Todd in the second quarter and ran right. Receiver Derrick Gaffney stayed home on the play to block Louis Breeden, which led to the Bengals cornerback buying in on the run. Gaffney then released, and McNeil slammed on the brakes to pass. When he looked up the field, Gaffney stood all alone at the 1-yard line. McNeil's pass found Gaffney's hands, and the Jets had their first touchdown.

Walton looked like a genius, and the Jets were on their way to a 44–17 win.

Such successes came into play when the Jets decided to make him the ninth head coach in team history in February 1983. Walton looked innovative, and he certainly had paid his dues on the football field as a player and a coach.

Good karma for Jets fans came in the fact that Walton grew up in Beaver Falls, Pennsylvania—Joe Namath's hometown—the son of a former NFL guard and coach, Frank "Tiger" Walton. Joe Walton became a good enough player during his years in Beaver Falls to earn a scholarship to the University of Pittsburgh. After achieving All-America honors at Pitt, Walton became a second-round choice of the Washington Redskins. He played four seasons for the Redskins before being traded to the New York Giants, where he played tight end for three years on Giants teams that reached the championship game three times but lost each time. He retired after the 1963 season, having caught 178 passes for 2,623 yards and 28 touchdowns during his seven seasons.

Climbing the coaching ladder, Walton became an assistant with the Giants in 1969 before moving to the Redskins in 1974. During those stints, Walton worked with Fran Tarkenton and Norm Snead on the Giants and with Joe Theismann on the Redskins. He went to the Jets in 1981 as the team's offensive coordinator and began another project in Todd.

Prior to Walton's arrival, Todd threw 30 interceptions in 1981. With Walton guiding Todd to the light, the Jets quarterback reduced his interception totals to 13, and the Jets put together a 6–3 season in strike-shortened 1982.

After the Jets went 2–1 in the 1982 postseason, Michaels suddenly announced his retirement and team president Jim Kensil hired Walton, who had already interviewed for jobs with the Atlanta Falcons, Kansas City Chiefs, and Los Angeles Rams.

Kensil pointed out the obvious reason for Walton's hiring when he said, "Well, you've seen the offense work in the games. He has good relations with the players. He will provide continuity for the franchise."

In Walton's initial remarks after becoming the Jets' new head coach, he promised the Jets would show "flair" and told reporters, "This is a good young football team just starting to reach its potential. We have a team capable of going to the Super Bowl."

Walton, who had gotten along well with Michaels, expressed that he tried to instill discipline in his players, but he also liked the idea of having fun. He also noted that he thought the Jets had just "scratched the surface" of where he expected the team's offense to go.

Based on the results Walton had gotten from the Jets' offense, which had an exciting array of young talent, Jets fans had reason to believe the team was entering a golden era under Walton.

After consecutive 7–9 seasons, the Jets went 11–5 and 10–6 in 1985 and 1986. In each of those seasons, they made the playoffs and lost. From there the Jets went mostly downhill before reaching the bottom, which came at the Meadowlands, where signs saying "Joe Must Go" adorned the stands during a 37–0 thrashing by the Bills in the final game of the 1989 season. The loss gave the Jets a 4–12 record for the season and led to Walton's firing three days later.

In seven seasons as the Jets' head coach, the team went 53–57–1 and lost two of the three playoff games in which they appeared.

78 Rich Kotite

Careful what you wish for, because, after all, what does one do when his dream comes true?

Rich Kotite found out the hard way that living the dream did not necessarily equate to happiness.

A Brooklyn native, the 52-year-old Kotite had been around the football universe before returning to his roots to become the 10th head coach in the history of the Jets.

Kotite had graduated from high school in Brooklyn, temporarily attended the University of Miami and then graduating from Wagner College in Staten Island before becoming a tight end and special teams player for the New York Giants in 1967. He went to the Steelers for the 1968 season and then returned to New York in 1969 to finish his playing career with the Giants, which concluded after the 1972 season.

In the years that followed, Kotite worked as an NFL assistant coach, including a stint with the Jets that began in 1983 as the team's receiver coach and culminated with him being the team's offensive coordinator, a stint that ended when head coach Joe Walton got fired. During Kotite's time with the Jets, he developed a relationship with owner Leon Hess.

Kotite followed Buddy Ryan as the Eagles' head coach, posting a 37–29 mark before getting fired after the Eagles went 7–9 in 1994; the team had begun the 1994 season 7–2.

Upon getting hired to coach the Jets, Kotite noted that a dream of his had come true. He and Hess were both confident that the fortunes of the Jets were about to turn around.

Said Hess of Kotite when he hired him, "I appoint Rich Kotite the leader, the coach to bring the Jets back. Richie's the leader of the Jets' family…. Rich is a fighter, a builder, a 'deze' and 'doze' guy, a leader, bringing the New York Jets back."

And Kotite offered that his team would be counted on to play with "the greatest determination" for 60 minutes, 16 games per season.

"I'm not a genius," Kotite told reporters. "I don't have all the answers. But if you have a team that you prepare, that plays hard for 60 minutes, you have a chance to succeed."

To say things did not turn out well would be a huge understatement.

With Boomer Esiason leading the offense, the Jets went 3–13 in Kotite's first season, 1995. During that season, the Jets were outscored 384–232 and their record was the worst in the NFL.

The following season Frank Reich and Neil O'Donnell made most of the starts at quarterback for a Jets team that managed to defeat only the Arizona Cardinals in Week 9 to finish with the worst record in team history at 1–15 as opposing teams outscored the Jets 454–279. Again, the Jets had the worst record in the NFL

Rich Kotite was not a very good coach. Here he looks sad watching his Jets get slaughtered 47–10 by the Raiders.

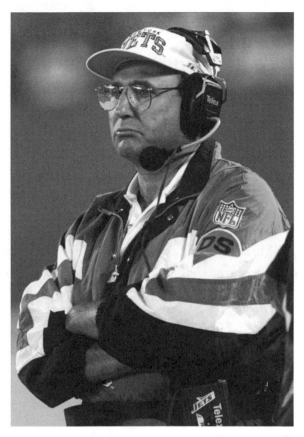

Kotite announced he had decided to resign his post two days before the final game of the season, which he did after coaching the Jets to a 31–28 loss to the Dolphins in the season's finale. In part, Kotite decided to step aside as a courtesy to his friend Hess, saving him from having to do the deed. Alas, the results Kotite and Hess had expected did not come to fruition.

Once Kotite stepped aside, the Jets were free to pursue Bill Parcells, who they eventually were able to bring in as the team's 11th head coach. Kotite did not coach in the NFL again after finishing with the Jets.

79 Bruce Coslet

The period leading up to the hiring of Bruce Coslet and his subsequent firing four years later ushered in one of the more bizarre periods in Jets football history. It was a period in which the management of the organization just couldn't get it right and repeatedly committed the sins of the past.

Joe Walton was dismissed as the team's head coach three days after the conclusion of the 1989 season. New general manager Dick Steinberg had done the firing, but he did not have a replacement ready to take over at the time of the firing, which led to a dog-and-pony show.

Michigan State coach George Perles became the first candidate publicly linked to the job, and the job would have been his had Michigan State allowed him to take the job. They did not, leaving egg on Steinberg's face.

By late January, Steinberg had a list of 11 candidates, among them Mike Holmgren, Bill Walsh's offensive coordinator for the highly successful San Francisco 49ers. Bruce Coslet's name was also on the list, and the 43-year-old offensive coordinator of the Cincinnati Bengals became the choice after dazzling Steinberg during his interview.

Coslet brought a lot of energy to everything he did.

He defied the odds after his college days as a tight end at the University of the Pacific by winning a spot on the Cincinnati Bengals roster in 1969. Though he never became a starter, the fire he played with on special teams earned him special teams captain honors. The 6'4", 227-pound native of Oakdale, California, played nine seasons for the Bengals, catching a modest 61 passes for 878 yards.

A tireless worker, Coslet ran a construction business during the off-seasons when he was a player before investing in a chain of delicatessens after his playing days concluded in 1976. He remained out of football until 1980, when the football bug finally got to him and he was hired by Bengals head coach Bill Walsh as an assistant for the special teams.

Eventually Coslet parlayed that start into the team's offensive-coordinator role when head coach Sam Wyche reluctantly handed over the team's offense to Coslet, who oversaw the Bengals' highly successful no-huddle offense that went to the Super Bowl at the end of the 1989 season.

Upon announcing that Coslet was the team's new head coach on February 6, 1990, Steinberg noted, "We needed a guy to change the environment."

In hindsight, the Jets were repeating what they had done when hiring Walton seven years earlier, as Walton had been the up-and-coming next-great-thing as the Jets' offensive coordinator.

Coslet announced an open competition between Ken O'Brien and Tony Eason for the starting quarterback job and noted that he did not need to make drastic personnel moves because any personnel could run the no-huddle. He also promised to bring in an aggressive, hard-charging defense, and he planned to serve as the team's offensive coordinator and call all the plays.

Unfortunately for Coslet and the Jets, nothing seemed to work, and he experienced a rash of misfortune, particularly in 1992 when he turned the offense over to second-year quarterback Browning Nagle, who flopped. That season also saw receiver Al Toon retire after suffering his fifth concussion, and defensive lineman Dennis Byrd broke his neck and was partially paralyzed, all of which brought many challenges to the Jets. The 1992 team finished with a 4–12 record.

The Jets traded for quarterback Boomer Esiason prior to the 1993 season in the hopes that reuniting Coslet and Esiason might bring back the spark they had shared together in Cincinnati. The move had modest results, but when the team needed to win the final game of the season to make the playoffs, they were routed 24–0 by the Houston Oilers.

After the season, Steinberg told Coslet he needed to relinquish his duties as the offensive coordinator and bring in someone else to call the plays. According to the accounts that followed, Coslet refused to do so. The Jets then fired Coslet—whose teams had gone 26–38—which led to the subsequent hiring of defensive coordinator Pete Carroll to become the Jets' head coach.

Coslet went on to become the head coach of the Bengals midway through the 1996 season, and he coached the team through the 1999 season.

Pete Carroll

Pete Carroll had greatness written all over him. Unfortunately for the Jets, Carroll's greatness would prove to be future greatness—long after he'd left the Jets.

Carroll came to the Jets as the team's defensive coordinator in 1990, joining new head coach Bruce Coslet, whom he had known since the age of 14. Four years later, Carroll became the coach of the Jets.

Carroll got to know Coslet when his brother played football at Pacific, as did Coslet. Carroll himself would later play football at Pacific before embarking on a coaching career that would see him work in assistant jobs at Arkansas, Iowa State, Ohio State, North Carolina State, and Pacific before heading to the NFL with the Buffalo Bills, Minnesota Vikings, and, finally, the Jets. Along the way he worked for Lou Holtz at Arkansas and Bud Grant with the Vikings. The time he spent with Grant had a particularly strong influence on him.

Carroll had never been a head coach anywhere when the Jets hired him after firing Coslet at the beginning of 1994. He experienced many emotions that day, as he suddenly would be ascending to his first head coaching position at the age of 42, but he would be taking his friend's job.

In hiring Carroll, the Jets felt they were getting a man who could boost the team with his youthful exuberance and vitality. The situation Carroll inherited was not ideal, given the fact that he lacked experience as a head coach, the team had finished above .500 just eight times in the previous 34 seasons, and he would be competing in a division with teams coached by the likes of Don Shula, Bill Parcells, and Marv Levy. Nevertheless, Carroll diligently attacked the position and tried to bring the team together. The initial results seemed to indicate that the Jets might have something in their charismatic and handsome new head coach.

The Jets began the 1994 season with a 23–3 win at Buffalo followed by a 25–22 win over the Denver Broncos in the home opener the next week. But the Jets lost their next three and then battled to remain at .500 until losing their final five games of the season to finish at 6–10.

The final game of the season was a 24–10 loss to the Houston Oilers, which gave them an 0–4 mark in December, which moved the team's December record since 1986 to 8–27.

Frustrated with the team's December legacy, Carroll noted to reporters after the final game of the season, "Not being able to change it is something we won't be able to forget for a long time."

Coinciding with the end of the season came the news that Dick Steinberg, the team's general manager, had been diagnosed with stomach cancer. Steinberg's health seemed to lessen his authority. So when he gave a vote of confidence to Carroll that he would be back for the next season, the power behind that vote felt hollow, which shortly thereafter proved to be the case.

Feeling that the team had quit, Leon Hess fired Carroll, saying, "The players, in my opinion, had the potential to go much farther than where they went. I unilaterally made the decision…. I owe it to Jets fans, to the Jets, and even to myself."

Carroll left the Jets to coach the San Francisco 49ers' defense and ended up getting a second crack at the NFL when he took over the New England Patriots job in 1997 and coached there through 1999. After the Patriots job, Carroll coached briefly with the Seattle Seahawks before taking over as the head coach at the University of Southern California after the 2000 season and found great success.

Carroll made the Trojans into a national powerhouse and continued to coach there until taking the position as head coach of the Seahawks after the 2009 season.

81 Tailgate at a Jets Game

Obviously, many Jets fans tailgate at the games already, but for those who have not, tailgating at a Jets game is a must. In order to offer a good perspective on the dos and don'ts, along with what to expect at a Jets tailgate, we went to Joseph Maino of TailgateJoe.com, who is an expert on such matters. Here is the Q&A that followed:

QUESTION: How would you describe the Jets tailgating scene?

TAILGATE JOE: Being that New York City is in the unique position of having two teams, you find the fans of each skewing toward a different demographic. On the average, Jets fans are younger and maybe a little rowdier than our Big Blew fan neighbors. This younger demographic is definitely evident in the tailgating vibe, which sees a lot of tailgaters showing up four hours earlier to have a great time enjoying food and a few beers with friends before the game.

Q: What do you believe are the best foods to cook or bring to the tailgate?

TJ: Due to restrictions on how long you can tailgate for at the stadium, the classic "slow and low" barbeque items don't work so well. The best things to bring to the stadium are fast-cooking, high-heat grill items. Since there are a large number of fans of Italian heritage, Italian-American dishes are always a crowd favorite, like sausage and peppers.

Q: Are there restrictions on when you can enter the park and what you can bring?

TJ: Unfortunately the NFL has tried to limit the amount of time tailgating can take place in stadiums in the league, and they have been pushing for four hours. The Jets and Giants haven't gone that extreme thus far but have capped it at five hours before game time. As far as what you can bring, the Meadowlands has always been pretty liberal with their tailgate policies. The one thing to know, though, is that if you do not have a parking pass to park in certain lots with the new stadium, you will not be allowed to tailgate. Thankfully, parking passes are usually pretty plentiful on the secondary market like StubHub. Also, there are always welcoming parties for those who do not feel like lugging coolers and grills with them, like the TailgateJoe.com parties that are open to all.

Q: What things should you avoid while tailgating?

TJ: In my years of experience tailgating with friends and running the TailgateJoe party, the one thing that should generally be avoided is hard alcohol; this just leads to problems. Stick to beer or wine....

Q: Do Jets fans show animosity toward fans of the other team?

TJ: We welcome all visiting fans to the TailgateJoe parties, and generally Jets fans are fine with visiting fans as long as the visiting fan doesn't get stupid and try to provoke confrontation. Obviously Patriots and Dolphins fans get it a little rough, but they are huge rivals, and Jets fans expect the same when visiting them. All in all, though, it is safe for a visiting fan to come out and see a game here.

Q: What kind of games do people play in the parking lots?

TJ: Like I said, Jets fans are generally younger, and the drinking games that were big in college are still big in the lot while tailgating. In recent years Beer Pong has taken off, and we even have some special custom tables at the TailgateJoe parties.

Q: How early should you get to the park?

TJ: You cannot enter until five hours before kickoff, and to ensure parking in the right lots, you should look to arrive three to four hours before kickoff.

Q: Does the partying/cooking/etc. continue after the games?

TJ: For some people it does, it just depends if you want to drag the coolers and stuff out and fire the grill back up.

Q: Is it a family atmosphere or more of a singles crowd?

TJ: There is a nice mix, and you can definitely fit in with either group. The new stadium promises lots of family friendly events and attractions before the game, and the single people definitely can find a good party. The TailgateJoe parties see lots of singles from early twenties to mid forties, both men and women.

Q: Any classic anecdotes you can share?

TJ: Back in the early 2000s, maybe around 2002, we used to do a smaller tailgate party near a very large party that no longer is around. Well, I went and found some Miami Dolphins piñatas and brought them along for the Miami game. I tied them to the bumper of my truck and, during the course of the tailgate, the animosity toward those piñatas kept growing. Finally, right before kickoff, someone procured a 2x4 piece of lumber, and we stuck the piñatas on the end of it and lit them on fire. We gave the Dolphins torch to our craziest friend, and he started running around the lot like a lunatic and ended up in the middle of that huge party next to us surrounded by 400 fans chanting J-E-T-S with the burning effigy. Of course that big party took the fire theme and started burning jerseys after that, but that is how the whole opposing-team-jersey burning started in the lots there.

Q: What is your best recipe for tailgating?

TJ: Hot dogs are a very serious thing in New York/New Jersey, with lots of the best hot dog stands in the country, so serving a good dog is key. My TailgateJoe hot dog chili is pretty awesome, kicks the crap out of any of that stuff they serve in Cincinnati or anywhere else, for that matter. [Grab the recipe at http://www.tailgatejoe.com/hot-dog-chili-topping/]

82. Watch *America's Game*

America's Game: The Super Bowl Champions is an NFL Films series of documentaries covering the winning team from every Super Bowl. The series first aired on the NFL Network in November 2006.

The quality of each episode makes watching them well worth any viewer's time, as they give a behind-the-scenes look at what happened on the road to the Super Bowl. And for any Jets fans, the episode that encapsulates Super Bowl III—narrated by Alec Baldwin—is a must-see, given some of the information that comes to light.

While there is the typical tribute to Joe Namath—how he guaranteed a Jets victory and went out and delivered—*America's Game* points out the obvious and what everybody who watched the Jets that season knew: the Jets were not a one-man team.

That team also had Emerson Boozer, Matt Snell, Johnny Sample, George Sauer Jr., and the list of names goes on and on for key players who contributed to the Jets' upset victory. While NFL Films obviously interviewed Namath for the documentary, they also interviewed wide receiver Don Maynard and defensive end Gerry Philbin, who had his finest season in 1968 when he accrued 14½ sacks.

Like any NFL Films production, the actual footage is splendid and does a nice job of bringing the 1968 season and Super Bowl III to life.

You might learn something new from Namath, and listening to him recount the greatest game in Jets history certainly is a part of what makes this worthwhile. Personifying Namath's being was a segment where he is on the *Kyle Rote Show* at the end of the 1968 season and he tells the host that he would prefer to play the Oakland Raiders instead of the Kansas City Chiefs for the AFL championship. You see a totally honest, forthright, and confident young man, who isn't afraid to speak his mind as he explains the reasons behind his thinking.

Meanwhile, Maynard is a colorful figure, and his insights and stories are terrific. But for the true Jets connoisseur, Philbin provides the main course.

Philbin is one of the best players in Jets history, and the native of Buffalo comes off as a secure man who is not afraid to speak candidly about Namath.

During the course of the documentary, Philbin speaks of Namath's less-than-stellar work ethic, and you get the feeling that Namath rubbed some teammates the wrong way. Players on the team recognized Namath's talents and were aware that they had a better chance of winning any time he played quarterback, but according to Philbin, neither Namath's talents nor his leadership qualities were reasons for him being elected to be a team captain. In an interview with Namath, Broadway Joe notes that one of the prouder moments of his career came when his teammates elected him a team captain. Seconds later, the camera shifts to Philbin, who maintains that Namath got elected as team captain at the instruction of the Jets' management, who coerced the players into electing Namath to the post in order to motivate him to become more responsible for his actions on and off the field and to work harder.

Jets fans will still love Namath after Philbin offers his recollections of what really happened, but they'll love Philbin, too.

Additionally, Jets fans should watch the *America's Game* for Super Bowl V, since it delves into how devastating the Colts' loss was in Super Bowl III and how they went about recovering from that loss to win Super Bowl V.

83 The Strange Season of Lou Holtz

Lou Holtz looked like the perfect guy to take over the Jets in 1976.

Judging from his success at North Carolina State, he obviously knew how to coach, and he had the personality to handle the media demands of New York City. What Holtz didn't have was the heart to coach professional football, as he'd already given his heart away to the college game.

After engineering four consecutive winning seasons at North Carolina State—where none of his teams lost more than four games—Holtz signed a five-year contract at the age of 39 to become the Jets' new head coach on February 11, 1976. The contract paid him approximately $75,000 per year, thereby making him one of the highest-paid coaches in the NFL.

The Jets were coming off their worst season in franchise history as they went 3–11 in 1975, yet Holtz appeared full of confidence about his abilities to get the job done and do so by employing the same approach he had used while coaching in college.

He told reporters, "I have faith in God, Lou Holtz, and the New York Jets, in that order."

The diminutive Holtz also told reporters there would be "no compromise" in some of the demands he would make of his players.

"They will have to execute fundamentals, and there will be discipline," Holtz told the *New York Times*. "I'm not, however, interested in harassment."

Finally, he noted that he would give himself three years to get the job done even though he had a five-year contract.

"If you don't do it then, you might as well pack it in, because the last two don't mean anything," he told the *New York Times*.

While all of Holtz's intentions sounded good, the college approach just didn't seem to work for the Jets.

The Jets were on the road for their first four games of the 1976 season, and they lost all four, including a 46–3 shellacking at Denver. Holtz's Jets won the home opener against the Buffalo Bills 17–14 on Pat Leahy's fourth-quarter field goal, which gave Jets fans a moment of hope before the team lost its next two games to move to 1–6 for the season.

Among the problems Holtz had to deal with was his quarterback situation, which consisted of a too-old Joe Namath and a too-young Richard Todd.

Midway through the season, Holtz began to contemplate stepping down from the Jets and taking over the head coaching job at the University of Arkansas, where his good friend Frank Broyles planned to step down as coach at the end of the season.

Holtz began to share his thoughts with reporters about Arkansas following a 37–16 Jets loss to the Redskins at Shea Stadium in Week 13.

After the initial salvo, the wavering began.

During the final week of the season, Holtz announced that he planned on honoring his commitment to the Jets and by doing so would remain the coach of the team. The following day, he announced his decision to resign, telling reporters, "God did not put Lou Holtz on this earth to coach pro football."

Holtz did not coach the Jets' final game of the season. Mike Holovak served as the team's interim coach during a 42–3 loss to the Cincinnati Bengals at Shea Stadium, which gave the team a 3–11 record for the season.

Holtz signed a five-year deal to take over at Arkansas, noting that he wanted "to find a place where I will be happy the rest of my life."

Holtz would coach the Razorbacks from 1977 through the 1983 season before stints at Minnesota, Notre Dame, and South Carolina.

84 Worst Team in Club History

The 1996 Jets own the dubious distinction of being the worst team in franchise history. So bad were the Jets that season that they became a regular punching bag for David Letterman's quips.

When Letterman's list was "Top 10 Signs That You Won't Be Receiving a Christmas Bonus This Year," the No. 1 reason on the list was, "You're the starting quarterback for the New York Jets."

And prior to the team's final game of the season, Letterman noted that the game would be televised—accompanied by a laugh track.

The road to that final game of the season proved tortuous for the Jets, who were led for most of the season by quarterback Frank

Reich. The veteran NFL quarterback threw 15 touchdowns for the season while also throwing 16 interceptions. Surprisingly, they had a 1,000-yard rusher in Adrian Murrell, who managed to run for 1,249 yards, averaging 4.1 yards per carry—no small accomplishment for a team that would win just one game. In doing so, Murrell became the first back to turn the trick since 1969 when Gale Sayers did it for the hapless Chicago Bears.

Rich Kotite coached this sinking ship that began the season with a 31–6 loss at Denver before returning home to lose to Indianapolis 21–7.

By the time they reached Phoenix to play the Arizona Cardinals in Week 9, the Jets had lost eight consecutive games to start the season. The Jets had a 24–14 lead in the fourth quarter when Rob Moore caught a six-yard touchdown from Kent Graham to pull the Cardinals to within three points of the lead. But Reggie Cobb's two-yard touchdown run gave the Jets a 31–21 lead that held, thereby ruining the Jets' chances for the antiperfect season.

Defying the early season forecasts for the playoffs seemed to be the mantra for the 1996 team that had loaded up for the season with the addition of $70 million worth of free-agent talent.

After defeating Arizona, the Jets got back on track by losing their next six games to leave the team one loss away from finishing the season winless, with a 1–15 record.

Heading into that final game, Kotite had already announced that he would be stepping down as the team's coach, which prevented owner Leon Hess from having to sully his hands to fire the coach, whose two teams had won a total of four games in two seasons while losing 27.

The Jets got off to a fast start in their 16th game of the season when Hugh Douglas bolted 62 yards with a fumble recovery to put the Jets up 7–0, and Murrell followed with a two-yard touchdown run to push the lead to 14–0.

After the Dolphins tied the game at 14, Kyle Brady hauled in an 11-yard touchdown pass from Glenn Foley to put the Jets back on top 21–14.

The Dolphins then put 17 unanswered points on the scoreboard to take a 31–21 lead. Wayne Chrebet hauled in a nine-yard touchdown from Reich to make the final score 31–28.

And just like that, a 1–15 season belonged to the Jets.

Attendance reached a milestone after the final game by having more than 200,000 "no-shows" for the season, which equated to approximately $5 million wasted for the no-shows.

By losing in the finale, the Jets joined four other teams in NFL history who compiled 1–15 records. The team finished ranked 27th in offense by scoring 279 points and 29th on defense by allowing 454 points.

Said Kotite, "Sometimes you work your tail off and things just don't work out. The buck stops here."

Fortunately for the Jets, Bill Parcells would become the team's next coach, drastically changing the fortunes of the team.

Walt Michaels

When Walt Michaels was named the coach of the Jets on January 4, 1977, he became the team's fifth coach in 15 months.

But in hiring the former standout for the Cleveland Browns and longtime AFL/NFL assistant, the Jets gained some semblance of stability, as he would serve in the position for the next six seasons.

Charley Winner began the Jets' parade of coaches with his 1975 exit, which brought Ken Shipp aboard to finish out the season in advance of Lou Holtz taking over for 1976. After Holtz resigned with one game remaining in the 1976 season, Mike Holovak took over before Michaels was hired after the season.

Michaels graduated from Washington and Lee, where he earned a bachelor of arts in psychology while playing fullback. After the Browns drafted him, they traded him to the Green Bay Packers, where he played for a season before getting traded back to the Browns in 1952. The move coincided with Michaels making a change of position to linebacker, which turned out to be good for the Browns and Michaels, as he excelled at the new position, earning All-Pro honors for four consecutive seasons while the Browns played in five NFL Championship Games and twice became champions.

Michaels had roots with the Jets from the early days of the AFL. He joined the team in 1963 and played in one game before accepting the defensive coordinator's position with the team, and he remained in the position until February 1973. That's when Jets coach Weeb Ewbank hired his son-in-law, Winner, and appointed him to be the Jets' next coach when he retired after the 1976 season. Frustrated about the decision, Michaels resigned and ended up becoming the defensive coordinator for the Philadelphia Eagles.

Michaels and the rest of the Eagles' staff were let go after the 1975 season, and Michaels returned to the Jets under Holtz, which put him in position to be the Jets' coach when Holtz made the surprise announcement that he would be leaving the job with four years remaining on his contract.

Under Michaels, the Jets went 3–11 his first season before going 8–8 in 1978 and 1979. The 1979 season also brought a memorable quip from Michaels, who addressed punter Chuck Ramsey's abilities by telling him in front of the team, "I can fart farther than you can kick."

Based on the back-to-back .500 seasons, Jets fans had great hopes for the 1980 season. But with Richard Todd running the show at quarterback, the team took a step backward, posting a 4–12 mark in a season that saw Todd throw 30 interceptions.

Michaels led the Jets to their best season under him the following year when they posted a 10–5–1 record before they finished 6–3 in the strike-shortened 1982 season. The 6–3 mark was good enough to put the Jets in the playoffs, where they defeated the Cincinnati Bengals and the Oakland Raiders before bowing out against the Miami Dolphins on a muddy field in Miami, one game away from a spot in the Super Bowl.

Michaels resigned after the season, offering the explanation that he needed a break from football. That opened the door for offensive coordinator Joe Walton to take over as head coach for the 1983 season.

Michaels resurfaced to coach the New Jersey Generals of the USFL for two seasons before he and his staff were fired by Donald Trump, the owner of the Generals.

Michaels never coached again in the NFL and later claimed that NFL owners had blackballed him from coaching in the league.

Play Jets Games

Looking for something fun to do with your Jets buddies, and you're burned out on the whole fantasy-football thing? There are several ways to go, and you don't have to spend a dime—save for maybe a few beers.

For starters, pick your own All-Time Greatest Team for the Jets.

Normally such duties fall to sportswriters, athletic clubs, and the like. But really, how much more do they know than you? They might talk to the players more and know what's going on inside their heads, but they're also up in the press box writing game stories, blogging, tweeting, or operating flipcams during the games, while you are simply watching the action. So why can't your team be as significant as one of the teams they pick?

Do you recognize Joe Namath as the team's all-time best quarterback, or do you go with Ken O'Brien or Mark Sanchez? How about defensive ends? Mark Gastineau certainly was the most glamorous, but was he one of the best? Certainly arguments can be made for Gerry Philbin, Verlon Biggs, and Joe Klecko. All-time greatest receiver? Has to be Don Maynard, or does it?

No doubt many conversations can be had haggling over who the best players are and why. In addition, there likely will be some debate about the most equitable way for you and your group to decide on the decisions that will represent your group, whether it's by unanimous vote, a majority vote, or a point system. No matter what the decision, picking your All-Time Greatest Jets Team will occupy the better part of an evening, at least, or it could take several meetings. So stock up your beer supply and prepare for some lively discussion.

Another Jets game is somewhat less complex but requires more memory, and that is the numbers game.

Procure a copy of a Jets media guide, which is complete with the all-time roster numerically. (Note: The media guide is for reference only.) You then begin with the No. 1 and proceed through No. 99, each player naming a player wearing the next number in the progression. For example, you name Mike Adamle for No. 1, and your friend names Raul Allegre for No. 2, and you do this all the way through No. 99—Mark Gastineau. You'd be surprised at how many players have worn each number, though the supply runs kind of short for Nos. 12 and 13. Only Namath, Al Dorow, and Harold Stephens wore No. 12, and only Maynard and Dave Jennings wore No. 13. Other than those numbers, you could go up and down the number list for quite some time.

Having a copy of a Jets media guide would also aid the playing of the second game, which is the alphabet game. Like the numbers game, you and a friend or friends take turns naming players. But in this game you do so alphabetically. You must understand the limitations of the game heading into it, which is the lack of any players with names beginning with a *Q*, *U*, or *X*.

All of the above-mentioned games are played without hooking up a game to your TV, and you don't have to draw pictures, stand on your head, or roll dice. In the end, you might actually learn something about your favorite team.

87 NFL's First Regular- Season Overtime Victory

After much debate, the NFL finally decided to change the rules by allowing for overtime games to take place during the regular season beginning in 1974.

Fans had embraced overtime games in the past with the 1958 NFL Championship Game being the biggest testament to the positive reaction to such games. The Baltimore Colts had defeated the New York Giants in sudden death, and many pointed to that game as the one that put the NFL on the map.

Once the new rule went into effect, the curious of mind began to wonder when the first regular-season overtime game would take place. The answer to that question came on September 22, 1974, at Denver's Mile High Stadium when the Denver Broncos and Pittsburgh Steelers played to a 35–35 tie in a crazy shootout. Ironically, a winner did not step forward that afternoon, despite the extra period.

Remember, the NFL added an overtime period for games that ended in a tie, but while sudden death was a part of the rule, it did not demand that a game be played until a team won the game. Playoff games had to have a winner because the postseason dictated that one team had to move forward. During the regular season, once the extra period ran its course, the game was finished whether a deadlock remained or not. Which is exactly what happened in the Broncos-Steelers game as the Steelers could be seen at the end of the overtime period running out the clock on their own 26, fearing what might happen if they threw caution to the wind.

And so the 1974 season went; no team had used the new rule to claim a win in overtime, which was the prevailing situation when the Jets played the New York Giants in a game at the Yale Bowl in New Haven, Connecticut.

Thanks to NFL schedule-makers, the Jets and Giants had met just once since the first time the merger took effect on the schedule in 1970. New Yorkers knew the two teams would not meet again until 1978 at the earliest.

Charley Winner was in the midst of his first campaign as the Jets' coach, and the team was off to a less-than-auspicious beginning at 1–7. The Jets looked like a far better team while battling the Giants to a 20–20 tie at the end of regulation. Amazingly, gimpy-legged quarterback Joe Namath scored the tying touchdown on a naked bootleg that saw him limp untouched into the end zone from three yards out. But the Jets also missed a field goal in regulation that would have won the game.

The Giants returned the favor in the overtime period, which gave Namath and the Jets the football.

Always a threat to throw deep, Namath did just that by hitting Rich Caster for a 42-yard gain on the Jets' first play of overtime. Namath then connected with Jerome Barkum to put the Jets at the Giants' 20.

After three running plays, the Jets moved the ball to the Giants' 5. The Giants stopped the Jets on first down before Namath faked a handoff into the line then spotted Emerson Boozer, who had found an opening behind linebacker Brad Van Pelt. Namath's pass landed solidly in Boozer's grasp, and the Jets had a 26–20 win, earning the Jets the distinction as the first team in NFL history to win a regular-season game in overtime.

The Jets seemed to gain some momentum from the victory, as they followed with victories in their final five games of the season to finish at 7–7.

88 Sing Lou Holtz's Jets Fight Song

Based on the geographic differences between the Minneapolis–St. Paul and the New York City–New Jersey areas, along with their cultural differences, one would expect the New York City–New Jersey area to win any contests involving celebrities or pop culture.

Generally that will always be the case, but not so where fight songs are concerned for their respective NFL teams. Prince came out with "Purple and Gold" for Minnesota Vikings fans to rally around, while Jets fans seem to be forever saddled with the remnants of a partial fight song composed by Lou Holtz.

Holtz, who came from the college ranks to coach the Jets in 1976, attempted to create a college football atmosphere for the Jets.

Holtz came aboard with the Jets and inherited a bad quarterback situation featuring soon-to-be-retired Joe Namath and the inexperienced Richard Todd, which seemed to only make Holtz long even more for the college game. After the Jets lost their first three exhibition games, the team traveled to Houston to play the Houston Oilers in the Astrodome.

In that game, Holtz had gotten peeved at Todd late in the game, which prompted him to pull Todd in favor of Namath, who

Lou Holtz grips a football during a news conference in New York after being named the new head coach of the New York Jets on February 10, 1976.

had already played. Since the game was only an exhibition, Namath had already removed all the bandages and braces from his knees. Nevertheless, he ran into the game, telling the other team's defensive line to please consider that all he planned to do was fall on the ball to run the clock out. Instead, Namath ended up fumbling, and the Oilers managed to move the ball into field-goal range, but Skip Butler missed from 35 yards out in his attempt to tie the score. Since the Jets won the game 27–24 and Namath did not get injured, Holtz felt rather chipper afterward, which led to the debut of "New York Jets Keep Rolling Along."

Holtz, who resembled a blonde-haired cross between Barney Fife and Woody Allen, had composed the song and figured that a victory brought just the right moment to break the news to his players that they now had a fight song. After all, didn't the Washington Redskins have "Hail to the Redskins"? And every college team known to man had a fight song.

Only, these were the Jets and not some college team.

In the locker room after the game, Holtz handed out mimeographed sheets on which were the words to the fight song he had written. He explained to all of his players that he expected them to sing the song after every win.

Can anybody picture Lombardi addressing the Packers in his postgame remarks about a song he'd penned?

A predictable response followed that included eyes rolled in disbelief at what their coach was asking them to do. But Namath stood up for his coach and chimed in when the singing began, thereby smoothing over what might have been an awkward moment.

On the plane back to New York, Holtz again handed out the sheets for everyone to sing, including the flight attendants and the writers who covered the team (who traveled with the team in 1976). Paul Zimmerman, who would later become *Sports Illustrated*'s famed Dr. Z, worked as one of the beat writers covering the Jets in 1976. Years later in an SI.com column, he wrote the following about that flight home: "Did I sing? You betcha, until the defensive coach, Walt Michaels, in the seat next to me, told me to shut the hell up."

Tragically, the full lyrics of the fight song seem to have gone the way of the missing scrolls of the Bible. Fortunately Jets fans can sing the following words of what could be recovered (as sung to the melody of "The Caissons Go Rolling Along"). So grab a beer or 10 and sing in harmony:

Win the game, fight like men,

We're together win or lose,

New York Jets go rolling along…

And where e'er we go,

We'll let the critics know

That the Jets are here to stay.

89 The First Thanksgiving

Harry Wismer appeared almost giddy when announcing the schedule for the fledgling New York Titans' first season. Next to the date for November 24, 1960—also known as Thanksgiving—was a Titans game against the Dallas Texans.

The Titans founder and president proclaimed that the game would become an annual Thanksgiving fixture for New York fans. Wismer's enthusiasm made the game sound as if it would trump the Macy's Thanksgiving Day Parade.

As the day drew near and the Titans prepped their 5–6 squad for the big game, a ceremony was staged at City Hall to designate the game as the "Mayor's Trophy" game. During the festivities, Wismer presented New York Mayor Robert F. Wagner with an autographed Titans football. And following the game, Mayor Wagner would present the silver cup to the winning team. The plan called for the score of each year's game to be inscribed on the trophy that stood 30" high.

In addition to the game holding significance for keeping the Titans' playoff hopes alive—despite having lost four straight—it would be their final home game of the season, and the game would be televised on ABC-TV, though blacked out locally.

Of note, tickets purchased to travel to the game on either of the two nonstop "football specials" operated by the Transit Authority would entitle each holder the opportunity to purchase a $4 ticket to the game at the Polo Grounds for $1.25.

Fans who showed up for the contest were treated to an exciting game.

Future Hall of Famer Don Maynard hauled in a 45-yard touchdown pass from Al Dorow to give the Titans a 7–0 lead. Roger

Donnahoo then scooted 57 yards with a fumble recovery to push the lead to 14–0.

Early in the fourth quarter, the Titans appeared to have a victory well at hand as they held a 34–13 lead. But the Texans managed to mount a comeback that saw them score three touchdowns in a seven-minute span. Once the Titans' lead had diminished to 34–28, the game seemed to be following a familiar script. The Titans had experienced the emptiness of not being able to hold leads several times during their inaugural season. No doubt the history of the Titans' first season inspired Dorow as he refrained from employing a conservative tact on offense. The Titans quarterback continued to throw the football and found Art Powell at the Texans' 2. Powell could not make the catch and pass interference was called. Fortunately for the Titans, Dewey Bohling then burst over the goal line for a two-yard touchdown, which enabled the Titans to take a 41–35 win.

Abner Haynes had done the most damage for the Texans, running the ball 11 times for 157 yards and two touchdowns. Meanwhile, Maynard and Art Powell worked their magic for the Titans, catching 18 passes for 289 yards. And Dorow completed 21 of the 33 passes he threw for 301 yards.

Wismer saw great things for the future of the game. Ever the visionary, Wismer no doubt looked at the attendance of 14,344 for that first game and figured that would be tripled in future years once the Titans gained the popularity he envisioned. And success did follow on the field, as the Jets won three consecutive Thanksgiving Day games before giving up the date in 1963.

Since 1962 the team has played only three times on Thanksgiving. The Jets lost to the Detroit Lions in 1972 and 1985—at Detroit. And in 2007 there was a renewal of sorts when the Jets lost to the Dallas Cowboys.

90 Attend a Game at the New Jets Stadium

Finally, the Jets have a real home, so any Jets fan needs to attend a game at the New Jets Stadium that opened in 2010.

Every year since the team began to play at the Polo Grounds, the Jets—and their fans to some extent—have felt like second-class citizens at their home ballpark, whether it was the Polo Grounds, Shea Stadium, or the Meadowlands. The Jets did not call the shots at the park and had little say so about what happened.

Over the years, the team's stadium situation led to many problems. For example, at Shea Stadium, the Jets often had to play their first few games of the season on the road in order to facilitate New York Mets games, and the Jets did not even receive parking revenues from their home games.

Fans might not get upset about who gets the parking revenues generated at their favorite team's games, but they should, because any revenues the team does not get can make them less competitive in trying to make player moves. Plus it can affect prices of tickets, merchandise, or concessions, or any number of consumer items at the ballpark, as the team needs to make up for the money they are not making. That won't happen at the New Jets Stadium.

Moving into New Jets Stadium, the Jets became 50-50 partners with the New York Giants, the team they shared Giants Stadium with that dictated what happened at the stadium.

Skanska won the design/build contract for the new stadium on January 26, 2007, and construction formally began with a ground-breaking ceremony on September 5, 2007.

Unlike the other homes of the Jets, game days give Jets fans the feeling of being in their home park due to the way the stadium is dressed in green with no traces of the other tenant visible.

The new park, which is 2,030,000 square feet, is larger than the Meadowlands, which was 900,000 square feet, and it includes an average concourse width of 40 feet at the new stadium as compared to 22 feet at the old. And capacity has increased from 80,254 to 82,500.

In addition, Jets fans will notice more turnstiles, premium elevators, escalators, parking spaces, three times the number of restrooms, and eight times the number of concession stands. And Jets fans can know that the players are happier in their new home since the home locker room boasts nearly 5,000 additional square feet of space.

For those fans desiring better seats, they are available at the New Jets Stadium in the form of club seating, which offers the best views and excellent access—including VIP reserved parking, a private club entrance into the stadium, and many other amenities and benefits.

Going to a Jets game at the New Jets Stadium is a truly enjoyable experience and nothing like what Jets fans have experienced at home games in the past.

For more information about the stadium, go to www.newjetsstadium.com.

91 Devastation in Cleveland

"High-flying" would have been an understatement for the way the Jets played in the first 11 games of the 1986 season.

In Joe Walton's fourth campaign as the head coach of the Jets, the team had won its opener at Buffalo against the Bills, returned home the next week to lose against the New England Patriots, and then rattled off nine consecutive wins to move to 10–1 for the season.

However, by that point of the season, the defense had been decimated. Just three players on the entire defense had started every game, so keeping key personnel healthy looked like an obstacle for defensive coordinator Bud Carson.

Still, the Jets' defense had allowed just 203 points, while the team's offense, led by Ken O'Brien—who was having a superlative season by completing nearly 67 percent of his passes to that point—had been responsible for most of the team's 303 points. Al Toon and Wesley Walker were O'Brien's primary targets and among the top receiving tandems in the NFL.

In Week 12, the Jets traveled to Miami to play their bitter rivals, the Dolphins, in a *Monday Night Football* showdown at the Orange Bowl. The Jets came away 45–3 losers, and their bubble seemed to have suddenly burst. From there the Jets stumbled through the remainder of the season to finish at 10–6.

Despite their finish, the Jets still managed to make the playoffs and defeat the Kansas City Chiefs 35–15 in the AFC Wild Card Game at the Meadowlands. By winning, the Jets earned a spot in the division playoff game against the Browns in Cleveland on January 3, 1987.

In the Browns, the Jets would be facing the team with the best record in the AFC at 12–4, but they had not won a playoff game since 1969, coming out on the losing end five times since. By this juncture, Pat Ryan had replaced O'Brien at quarterback and had played an errorless game against the Chiefs the previous week. And the Jets still had Freeman McNeil at running back, and he had become one of the best in the league.

Playing in an icebox known as Cleveland Stadium, the Jets took a 13–10 halftime lead as the wind from Lake Erie whipped through the grounds. McNeil scored from 25 yards out early in the fourth quarter to give the Jets a 20–10 lead and a taste in their mouths for the AFC Championship Game the next weekend. Just under five minutes remained in the game.

Marty Lyons made a Jets victory look even more probable when he sacked Browns quarterback Bernie Kosar on the first play of the Browns' next possession. Facing a second-and-20 situation on second down, Kosar threw incomplete, but inexplicably, Jets defensive end Mark Gastineau crashed into Kosar to earn a 15-yard penalty for roughing the quarterback. Kosar made the Jets pay by completing six of nine passes on a drive that culminated with a one-yard touchdown run by Kevin Mack just after the two-minute mark to cut the lead to 20–17.

The Jets got the ball back and were unable to get a first down, which forced them to punt with approximately 60 seconds remaining in the game. Kosar led the Browns to the Jets' 5 with time running out when he threw to Webster Slaughter in the end zone. Jets cornerback Russell Carter managed to knock down the pass, but he had a chance to make the interception and failed to do so, which enabled Mark Mosley's game-tying field goal that tied the game at 20 and sent the contest into sudden-death overtime.

In overtime, Mosley missed from 23 yards out to win the game before gaining redemption with a 27-yard field goal in the second overtime period to win the game, which lasted four hours and five minutes.

Cleveland went on to play the Denver Broncos in the AFC Championship Game and lost 23–20 in overtime thanks to some magic by Broncos quarterback John Elway.

92 Blair Thomas, the Jets' Biggest Bust

Blair Thomas even pleased the hard-to-please Jets fans when the Jets selected him with the second pick of the 1990 NFL Draft.

In past drafts the natives had gotten restless after the Jets picked the likes of Ron Faurot, Jeff Lageman, and Mike Haight, but this time you couldn't hear a peep from the nonbelievers. Simply stated: Thomas appeared to be a lock.

Even though the Penn State running back had suffered a knee injury during the 1988 season, the Jets had confidence—as did other teams—that he had made a full recovery. Evidence of his full recovery could be seen in his body of work compiled during the 1989 season, which culminated with a performance in the Holiday Bowl when he stomped through the Brigham Young defense to the tune of 186 yards. And he followed that performance with 137 yards on 11 carries in the Senior Bowl.

Thomas stacked a solid 195 pounds on his 5'10" frame, clocked a 4.48 in the 40, and came from a solid football program with the Nittany Lions, for whom he had a career average of 5.4 yards per carry. He finished second on Penn State's career-rushing list with 3,301 yards, leaving him 97 yards short of Curt Warner's top spot.

So confident were the Jets that Thomas would step right into the lineup without any problems that they issued him No. 32, which to some was a sacred Jets number, because hard-nosed Emerson Boozer had worn it.

By using the second pick of the draft to select Thomas, the Jets made him their highest pick since they selected Johnny "Lam" Jones with the second pick in 1980.

A bad omen came when Thomas missed 34 days of training camp while negotiating his contract. Upon signing a six-year, $15

Johnny "Lam" Jones

In the 1976 Summer Olympics in Montreal, Johnny Jones brought home a gold medal from running the second leg in the 4 x 100 meter relay.

He would use that speed to become a football star at the University of Texas, where he also acquired the nickname "Lam" from Texas coach Darrell Royal because he was from Lampasas, Texas, while the team had another Johnny Jones, who hailed from Hamlin, Texas, whom Royal dubbed "Ham."

Lam eventually moved from running back to wide receiver for the Longhorns, and the move paid off big for Jones, who could run a 4.3 in the 40. The Jets already had speedster Wesley Walker at the time, but they fell in love with the idea of spreading the field out with blazing speed at receiver on both sides. Having decided that Jones would be the guy to give the team a double-edged sword, the Jets had to get into position to draft the speedster. So they sent two first-round picks to the San Francisco 49ers for the No. 2 overall selection in the 1980 NFL Draft. Detroit selected Oklahoma running back Billy Sims with the first pick, which allowed the Jets to nab the 5'11", 180-pound Jones with the second pick.

Jones had a promising start in his rookie season when he caught 25 passes for an average of 19.3 yards per reception while catching three touchdowns, all of which came in the final five games of the season. Unfortunately for Jones and the Jets, his performance went downhill from there.

Injuries played a big part of Jones' demise as he played in just 23 games over the course of the 1981 and 1982 seasons. He managed to have his best season in 1983 when he caught 43 passes for 734 yards, which included the best performance of his career when he caught seven passes for 146 yards and a touchdown against Pittsburgh.

While injuries and substance abuse took their toll on Jones, the biggest problem for the speedy receiver was the fact that he dropped a lot of passes. He spent his entire five-year career with the Jets, catching just 32 passes while playing in eight games in 1984.

million deal, Thomas told reporters, "I'll put it this way: I think I can afford to take my linemen out to dinner."

Thomas continued to fuel the hype by running for a three-yard touchdown in his first carry as a Jet in the team's final preseason game before the 1990 season.

Perhaps too much was expected of Thomas and that's why he's considered such a bust. But the difference between what had been expected of him and what he delivered indeed was considerable.

The strained hamstring he suffered prior to the Jets' 1990 season opener appeared to be a precursor of things to come. Though he managed to play in the opener, he was far from spectacular as he carried the ball five times for 13 yards in a 25–20 loss against the Bengals in Cincinnati. He did better the following week in a 24–21 win over the Cleveland Browns when he gained 46 yards on six carries. He gained 203 yards in the team's next four games as the Jets lost two of three. By the end of his rookie season, he had run for 620 yards. Not bad, but far short of his lofty expectations.

By the time Thomas carried the ball for his last time during the 1993 season, he had run for 2,009 yards on 468 carries and five touchdowns in four seasons. He left the Jets as an unrestricted free agent prior to the 1994 season believing the problem had been in the way the Jets had used him.

"Coming out of Penn State, they knew the kind of back that I was," Thomas told the *New York Times*. "They knew I needed to get the ball a lot. In a game, most backs get better and stronger the longer they play. Most of the big gains come late in the game when you've worn down the defense."

Thomas would play for three more teams over the course of the 1994 and 1995 seasons before his career came to an end.

And the biggest bust in Jets history sailed off into obscurity.

93 Winner Is a Loser

Weeb Ewbank knew the time was drawing near to retire from coaching when the calendar turned to 1973. Since the longtime Jets coach remained the team's general manager, he felt the right move for him would be to announce that he would retire following the 1973 season. By doing so, Ewbank orchestrated the signing of his successor, 47-year-old Charley Winner, who also happened to be Ewbank's son-in-law, to a three-year contract.

The Jets veiled the decision as being that of Jets president Phillip H. Iselin, but most could see through why the decision had been made.

Winner had been an aide to Ewbank for nine years when Ewbank coached the Baltimore Colts. He went on to coach the Cardinals from 1966 through 1970 before being dismissed with a 35–30–5 record, which included some racial discord during his tenure.

Winner served as an assistant coach with the Washington Redskins in 1972 before accepting a job with the Jets as an assistant coach in 1973 in advance of his takeover in 1974.

Winner was married to the former Nancy Ewbank, one of Weeb's three daughters, and spoke after his hiring as if the family connection had no bearing on the decision to make him the team's coach-in-waiting.

"My wife and I knew what people would say," Winner told the *New York Times* after the news became public. "I don't want to be Weeb's coach. Phil assured me that I'm his coach, not Weeb's coach."

Regardless of how the package was wrapped, the Jets were getting Ewbank's son-in-law, much to the chagrin of defensive coordinator Walt Michaels, who had operated under the belief that he would be the team's head coach once Ewbank retired. Subsequently, Michaels, who had been with Ewbank and the Jets for 10 seasons, left the staff.

The Jets had finished the 1973 season with a 4–10 mark, which made Winner's first year at the helm in 1974 resemble a nice turnaround. With Joe Namath starting 14 games, the Jets got 20 touchdowns from their oft-injured quarterback, while John Riggins and Emerson Boozer combined to rush for over 1,100 yards as the Jets went 7–7 in Winner's first campaign. The team finished the season with six straight wins, which fueled high hopes for the 1975 season. But midway through the 1975 season the good feelings from having Winner as the coach had diminished.

The Jets had won four of their five exhibition games, spurring talk that the team would again go to the Super Bowl. Then they got walloped 42–14 in their opening game against the Buffalo Bills, which seemed to set the tempo for the season.

Early in November 1974, the Jets lost 24–23 to the Bills after deciding not to kick a 36-yard field goal late in the game that would have given the Jets a nine-point lead. After the attempt to go for it on fourth down failed and the Bills came back to take a one-point win, Winner became fair game for second-guessers.

The loss prompted questions about whether Winner would be back for the 1976 season to finish the third and final year of his contract. Iselin responded to those questions by saying that Winner would be back no matter how poorly the Jets finished the season. In other words, Winner received the dreaded "vote of confidence" perceived by many as a precursor for being fired.

Then, 16 days later—with the team in the midst of a six-game losing streak—the axe fell on Winner, and Jets quarterback coach Ken Shipp was named the interim head coach. About his decision to fire Winner, Iselin explained, "To save Charley and to save the team, we had to do it now."

Winner coached just 23 games for the Jets, posting a 9–14 mark. When the Jets fired him they had a record of 2–7; they finished the 1975 season 3–11.

94 Woody Johnson

Woody Johnson officially became the owner of the Jets on January 11, 2000, when his bid was approved to purchase the team from the estate of Leon Hess. Under his ownership, the Jets entered a new era in which nothing but first class would be acceptable for the team and its fans.

Johnson's family had founded Johnson & Johnson, and his father had served as president of the company. Though he did not follow him into the ivory tower of the worldwide healthcare company, he did attain much of his wealth through ownership of stock in the company. He also had owned and sold a cable-television company and ran a personal-investment company. All of this added up to financially enable him to buy the Jets for the price of $635 million. His winning bid topped the $612 million bid by Charles Dolan, the chairman of Cablevision, which owns Madison Square Garden, the New York Knicks, and the New York Rangers.

Johnson brought with him a great appreciation for Jets fans. To his way of thinking, the fans were the foundation for any successful team, and since becoming owner, he has acted accordingly. Unlike Hess, who operated almost as a recluse, rarely making public appearances, Johnson's face became well known to Jets fans.

Tailgaters in the Jets' parking lot have grown accustomed to seeing the team's owner walking through to meet and greet fans

Atlantic Health Jets Training Center

On September 2, 2008, the Jets officially moved into their new home at the Atlantic Health Jets Training Center in Florham Park, New Jersey.

This completed a process that began on March 31, 2006, when the Jets announced they would relocate their training center from their longtime Long Island base to Florham Park. Construction began in April 2007.

Jets owner Woody Johnson was pleased with the final product and he called the new facility "the most beautiful site on the face of the earth for a football team."

Upon seeing the facility, New Jersey governor Jon Corzine added, "What a place. I think I'm about to do a 'J-E-T-S! Jets! Jets! Jets!'"

Housed on the 27 acres is the 224,000-square-foot complex that provides a state-of-the-art learning, practice, and working environment for the coaches, staff, and players.

On the grounds are five full-length fields. Three of the fields are natural grass, one is a Sportexe synthetic turf field outdoors and the other is a Sportexe synthetic turf in the indoor field house. Each field has a permanent scoreboard.

Personifying the flexibility of the complex—which allows the team to maximize what can be done on the grounds—are goalposts that can be repositioned 90 degrees to accompany practices.

Throughout the complex are over 75 miles of data cabling.

Treating the players in a fashion that will help draw players to the team in the future was a priority when building the 5,500-square-foot locker room and the almost 11,000-square-foot weight room.

In addition, there are 10 classrooms and two individual study rooms that are in close proximity to the practice fields.

Inside the building are 60 large-screen TV monitors. And in the Players Gallery, a life-size photo of cheering Jets fans spans the building's main corridor, which is in place to remind the players and the entire organization about the importance of the fans.

Not only is the facility top-shelf, but it is convenient, as Newark Liberty International Airport and the Meadowlands are short drives away.

The Atlantic Health Jets Training Center should serve the team well for many years to come and will no doubt be an attractive selling point for enticing players to join the team.

while also soliciting feedback about the organization. In addition to making the fans feel special, he has made the athletes wearing Jets uniforms feel special and appreciated as well. Much of this has been derived from his approach to giving the team more than what it needed to become a winner.

Included in this pursuit has been the move into Atlantic Health Jets Training Center, a state-of-the-art practice facility and head-quarters. And there is a new stadium as well. Shortly after buying the Jets, Johnson had grandiose plans to relocate the team to a venue known as West Side Stadium in Manhattan. Subsequently, that project met its demise, prompting Johnson to announce that his team would accompany the New York Giants to a new stadium

Jets owner Woody Johnson before a preseason game against the St. Louis Rams on August 14, 2009, at Giants Stadium.

in the Meadowlands. He came through on that promise and moved the team into a new stadium in the fall of 2010.

Johnson has been involved in charitable organizations for most of his adult life. Among his causes have been the prevention, treatment, and cure of autoimmune diseases, in particular lupus and diabetes, after one of his daughters was affected with lupus and another with diabetes. Johnson has served as a trustee of the Robert Wood Johnson Foundation, which is the nation's largest philanthropic organization devoted to health and health care. Having that background no doubt inspired his feeling that the organization needed to give back to the community in the way of promotion of youth fitness and various charities through the Jets charitable foundation, which has raised millions of dollars to date.

In Johnson's first 10 seasons as owner of the team, the Jets posted seven winning seasons and appeared in nine postseason games, capturing an AFC East title in 2002.

Johnson is well respected by other NFL owners, which led to his being a part of the commissioner search committee that worked to find a replacement for NFL commissioner Paul Tagliabue. That committee came up with his successor in Roger Goodell.

In short, Johnson is an owner the fans feel good about guiding their team.

95 Read Keyshawn's Book

Want a little insight into why the Jets were once a really bad team? Get yourself a copy of *Just Give Me the Damn Ball!: The Fast Times and Hard Knocks of an NFL Rookie.*

Keyshawn Johnson was the No. 1 overall selection of the 1996 draft and joined a Jets team coached by Rich Kotite that went 1–15 in Johnson's rookie season.

The book chronicles Johnson's rookie season, in which he caught 63 passes and spent a lot of time figuring out what everybody else on the team did wrong.

Go behind the scenes with Johnson, who recounts in more than candid fashion the road to becoming the top pick of the draft from his days as a premier high school and college star at USC to his rookie season when the 6'4" receiver was supposed to be the player who would turn around the Jets' fortunes.

Part of the book deals with what it's like to be 23, playing in the New York market, and viewed as some kind of savior for a football team that has a lot of moving parts. Johnson deals with the frustration of losing and seemingly has clarity about everything that went wrong with the Jets during their disastrous 1996 season and frustration about why nobody else in the organization can see what he sees as obvious problems that need fixing.

Johnson comes off as brash and almost arrogant in finding a lot that is wrong with other people, and he doesn't mind putting his thoughts in an unkind—though often funny—way. And where warts are concerned, Johnson never takes a look in the mirror. However, you do see a man who, despite his hubris of writing a book during his first season in the league, is passionate about winning.

Amid all the bravado, Johnson manages to disarm the reader with some of his boasts, such as boldly proclaiming that he is the best receiver of all time. Based on the end results of his 11-year NFL career, of which he spent four years with the Jets, Johnson proved to be a pretty good receiver but hardly the best of all time.

Just imagine being one of Johnson's teammates and reading some of the things he had to say about the team. There is no way he won any popularity contests after this book—coauthored by Shelley Smith of ESPN—was published.

In the book, Johnson comes up with a conspiracy theory about a pregame injury to Neil O'Donnell in which the Jets quarterback pulled a calf muscle warming up prior to the Jets' 13th game of the season. The conspiracy involved Kotite and offensive coordinator Ron Erhardt.

Johsnon wrote, "How do you pull a calf muscle tossing a football around? Half of me says the dude was faking it so that Erhardt and Kotite could keep their jobs. It gave them a big fat excuse as to why we were terrible. They could say, 'Hey, we haven't had the $25 million man [O'Donnell]. How are we supposed to win?' I think he went down, maybe not to save Kotite but definitely to save his guru, old man Erhardt."

Kotite got fired and Bill Parcells took over the Jets prior to the 1997 season, retaining Erhardt. Johnson's book brought enough controversy to the Jets' camp in the fall of 1997 that there were concerns about whether O'Donnell and others would get over some of the things Johnson wrote.

Apparently they managed to find a way to get along during the 1997 season, as O'Donnell started 14 of 16 games and Johnson caught 70 passes as the Jets compiled a much-improved 9–7 record.

96 Watch the 1965 Orange Bowl

When told to watch the 1965 Orange Bowl, the first inclination for any Jets fan might be to ask, "Why the heck would I want to do that?"

The answer is that it is quality viewing for any Jets fan wanting to see several of their biggest future stars playing in a huge college bowl game before they wore the green and white.

Texas played No. 1 Alabama that night at the Orange Bowl in Miami. Alabama had already been recognized as national champions before the game was played, a custom that was changed in 1965. Another historic note was that the Orange Bowl was moved to a prime-time slot on network television for the first time. Once the game was finished, that decision would be validated many times over.

Among the players playing were Joe Namath, who made his final appearance for legendary Alabama coach Paul "Bear" Bryant. The Jets had already selected Namath with the first pick of the American Football League Draft back in November 1964. Also playing in the game was George Sauer Jr., who was a receiver for Texas and the son of George Sauer Sr., the team's director of player personnel; he had already been drafted by the Jets too, even though he had a year of eligibility left for the Longhorns. Future Jets safety Jim Hudson played for Texas, and future Jets linebacker Paul Crane played for Alabama.

Namath, who had suffered a knee injury prior to the game, did not start for Alabama, and most figured he would not play in the game. Who knows what might have happened had he started for the Crimson Tide that night?

Texas jumped on Alabama early. Ernie Koy, who New Yorkers remember because he played six seasons for the New York Giants, took a handoff on a sweep and ran 79 yards for a touchdown. Hudson, who had missed most of the 1964 season with a knee injury, then found Sauer wide open for a 69-yard touchdown pass to put Texas up 14–0 in the second quarter.

Alabama looked like they might get blown out, but Namath's backup, Steve Sloan, got hurt in the first half, which paved the way for Namath to enter the game in the emergency situation.

"Vintage Namath" is the best way one can describe what happened next. The senior quarterback set an Orange Bowl record by completing 18 of 37 passes for 255 yards and two touchdowns.

All-American Texas middle linebacker Tommy Nobis said of Namath, "I've never been so scared. Namath was great. I was scared the whole second half."

Added Texas' defensive backs coach, "[Namath is] the best I've ever seen. I'd hate to see him on two good legs."

Namath won MVP honors, but Alabama did not win the game, as Texas managed to stop the Crimson Tide on fourth down at the Longhorns' 1-yard line late in the game. Namath tried to sneak the ball in, and Nobis stuffed the play to preserve the victory.

Bryant would later talk about the goal-line stand when he told *Sports Illustrated*, "Our guys thought he scored. Afterward, one of the writers asked me who called the play. I said I had (I always call the ones that don't work). He said, 'How can a $12,000-a-year coach call the plays for a $400,000 quarterback?' I admitted he had a point."

Namath, of course, would sign a $400,000 contract to play for the Jets.

97 Championship Defense

Joe Namath is the man synonymous with the Jets' first (and only, through 2009) championship season, but the Jets' defense that year proved to be the backbone.

Walt Michaels, who would later become head coach of the team, served as the team's defensive coordinator and he had plenty of talent to work with in trying to stop the other team's offense.

The Jets used a standard 4-3 defense.

On the defensive front they had Gerry Philbin and Verlon Biggs at the ends and Paul Rochester and John Elliott at the tackles.

Linebackers included Ralph Baker and Larry Grantham on the outside with Al Atkinson in the middle. Johnny Sample and Randy Beverly were the cornerbacks, and Jim Hudson and Bill Baird were the safeties.

In short, with that collection of talent, the Jets' defense could pretty well play straight up against any offense without any tricks or gimmicks included. And they were quite effective.

In 14 games, the Jets' offense scored 419 points while the stingy Jets' defense allowed just 280, making for a significant point differential of 139 points. Additionally, the Jets finished the season a positive-15 in the turnovers department—which also served as a compliment to the team's offense.

By the end of the 1968 season, the Jets' defense led the AFL in total rushing yards allowed with just 1,195.

Once the Jets had earned their way into the Super Bowl, the talk began regarding what the high-powered offense of the Baltimore Colts, led by Earl Morrall, was going to do to the Jets' defense. Unlike the Jets' quarterback, who opted to break the athletes' code by talking about how the Jets were going to beat the Colts, the defense sat back and waited for the game when their actions would do the talking for them.

Colts tight end John Mackey, who was the prototype for a generation of hard-blocking, pass-catching tight ends who could run with the football, was the one player on the Colts' offense the Jets feared. So they double-teamed him with the idea that if they could stop Mackey, they could stop the Colts' offense. Meanwhile, the Jets' linebackers focused on stopping the Colts' running attack, while the cornerbacks dealt with the Colts' receivers with single coverage. And the plan worked.

While running back Tom Matte did accrue 116 yards against the Jets, making him the lone running back to surpass 100 yards against the Jets' defense all season, the rest of the Colts' attack came up empty.

The Jets' defense intercepted the Colts four times during the game. Beverly had two while Hudson and Sample had one each in the 16–7 Jets win. By holding the Colts to one touchdown, the Jets held the Colts to their lowest point total in 35 games, and the Jets' plus-four turnover margin in the game saw the Jets finish with a run of 11 games in which they had a plus-25 turnover margin.

After the Jets had finished taking care of business against the Colts, Johnny Sample, who had played for the Colts, told the *New York Times*, "When Earl Morrall released the ball, our defensive backs were racing to the ball. We read him pretty good. And I'll tell you, I feel pretty good. I've been thinking about this game for three years—every day."

Jets running back Emerson Boozer summed up the day succinctly by saying, "It was our defense. Our defense broke their backs."

History will remember the offense of the 1968 Jets, but those who played knew the true story: the Jets had one solid defensive unit.

Bulldog Turner

Second- and third-place finishes weren't good enough for the Titans in their first two seasons, so Harry Wismer, team owner and president, made a coaching change prior to the 1962 season by bringing in Bulldog Turner.

The former NFL great replaced another NFL great in Sammy Baugh, the Titans' first coach, who still had a year remaining on his contract when Turner took over the job. Typical of the mess that the organization was at the time, Baugh wasn't simply fired and paid

Clyde "Bulldog" Turner, center for the Chicago Bears, at training camp in Rensselaer, Indiana, on August 8, 1946.

the remaining amount on his deal; rather the Titans kept him as a consultant for the team at his $20,000-a-year salary.

The week prior to Turner being announced as the new coach in December 1961, Wismer threatened to demote Baugh from head coach to assistant. Baugh didn't blink an eyelash when responding to said threat, as he told the *New York Times*, "That's wonderful. I'd like to be an assistant at these prices."

Turner signed a two-year deal to coach the team and made it clear he would welcome having Baugh become one of his assistants; Baugh declined.

During his playing days from 1940 to 1952, Turner had been a standout linebacker and center for the Chicago Bears, making

Gilchrist Rumbles over Jets

Passing records established in a single game can easily be indicative of a win or a loss, but it's rare when an individual rushing record is set in a game where losing accompanies the feat. When Cookie Gilchrist of the Buffalo Bills stormed through the Jets on December 8, 1963, to establish a single-game rushing mark against the Jets, a lop-sided victory by the Bills followed.

A crowd of 20,222 at Buffalo's War Memorial Stadium watched as the 251-pound fullback had his finest day as a professional.

Gilchrist had led the AFL in rushing in 1962 with 1,096 yards, and the Bills' game plan heading into the contest with the Jets was simple: have quarterback Daryle Lamonica hand the football to the 28-year-old fullback.

Making matters worse for the Jets was the fact that Jets quarterback Al Wood got injured on the first snap he took in the game and did not return. After that, the day turned into a highlight reel for Gilchrist.

He capped a 24-yard touchdown drive with a four-yard run in the first quarter to put the Bills up 7–0. Gilchrist scored again on a three-yard dive early in the second quarter.

Shortly after the intermission, Gilchrist gained 67 yards on an 87-yard Bills drive culminated by his third touchdown on a one-yard run. He went on to score touchdowns on 19- and six-yard runs to give him five for the day.

Calculating Gilchrist's rushing totals for the day was no easy task, but once the final gun sounded and the Bills had a 45–14 win, those numbers were tallied, and they were astounding. In 36 carries, the bruising Gilchrist gained 243 yards and five touchdowns.

The yardage total set an AFL record, while the five touchdowns tied a record set by Billy Cannon and Abner Haynes.

Despite the outstanding day and the boost to his yardage total for the season, Gilchrist did not surpass 1,000 yards for the 1963 season and never surpassed the season mark again in his six-year career.

All-Pro six times while helping to lead the Bears—also known as "the Monsters of the Midway"—to four NFL championships. He played college football at Hardin-Simmons University and was the Bears' first-round pick in the 1940 NFL Draft.

Turner also acquired a reputation as a coach on the field while playing for the Bears, which led to him becoming an assistant coach under legendary Bears coach George Halas after the 1952 season and serving in that capacity through 1958.

Upon taking the reins of the club, Turner declared he would run a spread formation on offense to a degree that the team's level of talent would allow. His arrival brought freshness to the team in contrast to Baugh, who had cut the figure of a coach whose only priority was to cash a paycheck. Turner told the media that he would run the team the way he thought it should be run, which meant that he would not adhere to anything Baugh did unless he thought it made sense.

"In 25 years of contact with the game, I have gotten into the winning habit, and I'm far too old to change now," Turner said.

To that end, Turner came up with a new playbook that he boasted of that was 250 pages in length.

The Titans attempted to gain a higher profile, which included Turner and Wismer both claiming that they could beat the New York Giants, their crosstown NFL rivals. The Titans even issued a challenge to the Giants in January 1963 that they would play a game against each other for charity. Of course the challenge met deaf ears in the Giants camp.

Eventually all of the extra energy Turner brought to the job came up empty in New York. Attendance tanked, and Wismer ran out of money, which meant the players were not getting their checks. At one point, the players made a decision that they were not going to play in the team's November 22, 1962, game against the Denver Broncos. Turner stepped in to promise the players they would be paid. They believed their coach and went out and beat the Broncos 46–45 at Denver.

The Titans finished the year at 5–9. Wismer had to sell the team after the season, and the new ownership group headed by Sonny Werblin fired Turner and brought in Weeb Ewbank.

Turner was elected to the Pro Football Hall of Fame in 1966 and his No. 66 was retired by the Bears.

Al Groh

Bill Parcells stepped down as the coach of the Jets early in January 2000, and his replacement, Bill Belichick, resigned a day later before really taking over the job, thereby earning the Jets the unique distinction of having two ex-coaches in two days.

Two weeks later the Jets named 55-year-old Al Groh as the new coach of the team. While the Jets looked scorned after the way Belichick walked away from his deal, Parcells had actually recommended Groh for the job; he had more than paid his dues and had the résumé to assume the job.

Groh was born in New York City and grew up in Manhasset, New York, before attending the University of Virginia, where he played defensive end for the football team and defense for the lacrosse team.

Groh's first college coaching job was at Army, which is where he worked with Parcells for the first time. He moved from West Point to become the head freshman football coach at Virginia, from which he progressed to become the varsity coach of the Cavaliers' defensive line. He moved to North Carolina, then back with Parcells at Air Force before coaching at Texas Tech. Wake Forest hired him as their head coach in 1981, and he coached the Demon Deacons through 1986.

Groh's first year in the NFL coaching ranks came in 1987 as the special-teams and tight-ends coach for the Atlanta Falcons. He returned to college briefly at South Carolina, then joined the New York Giants as their linebackers coach in 1989. He became the team's defensive coordinator in 1991. After a stint with the Cleveland Browns, Groh joined up with Parcells again with the New England Patriots before he took over as the Jets' linebackers coach from 1997 to 1999.

By the time Groh was hired as the Jets' coach, he had worked off and on with Parcells for 13 years. Included in those stints were coaching for two Super Bowl teams in the Giants, who won Super Bowl XXV, and the Patriots, who lost Super Bowl XXXI.

With Groh at the helm, the Jets got off to a stellar start in 2000 by reeling off wins over the Green Bay Packers, the Patriots, the Buffalo Bills, and the Tampa Bay Buccaneers to take over first place in the AFC East with a 4-0 mark. But the team experienced a three-game losing streak in the middle of the season and lost their final three games to finish at 9–7 and miss making the playoffs. The Jets scored 321 points and allowed 321 points in 2000.

Though Groh had proved to be a solid coach in his NFL head coaching debut, Jets fans never really got the chance to know him, because after the 2000 season he left the Jets to take the head coaching job at Virginia when longtime coach George Welsh resigned after 19 seasons.

Had the Virginia job not been Groh's dream job, he would have remained the Jets' coach, and who knows what might have happened? He told reporters that the decision to leave the Jets had been a difficult one, but those close to him had impressed upon him that the Virginia job was what he'd always wanted. So he left the Jets with three years remaining on his contract.

Groh coached at Virginia through the 2009 season, when he was fired from the position after the final game of the season that saw the Cavaliers lose to in-state rival Virginia Tech. He went on to take the defensive coordinator position at Georgia Tech in 2010.

Marty Lyons

Heading into the 1979 NFL Draft, Jets coach Walt Michaels made it clear what he wanted by expressing a desire to extract a defensive lineman who could improve the team's pass rush. So when the time came for the Jets to make their first selection with the 14th pick of the first round, they went for Marty Lyons, a 6'5", 250-pound left tackle from the University of Alabama.

Lyons had been an All-American at Alabama and part of the Crimson Tide's 1978 National Championship team. Alabama fans would always remember him for his part in helping the Alabama defense make a goal-line stand against Ohio State in the Sugar Bowl to help win the title.

The Jets also selected Mark Gastineau in that draft, so without a doubt, the Jets managed to improve their pass rush in 1978.

Lyons had been the main guy the Jets wanted in the draft, and he would prove them correct in the coming years while wearing No. 93 in the green and white and becoming a fixture at defensive tackle, nose tackle, and defensive end. While Lyons had strong pass-rushing skills, he did his best work playing the run.

Never flashy, Lyons brought consistency to his profession, and he combined with Abdul Salaam, Gastineau, and Joe Klecko to form the famed New York Sack Exchange that led the NFL with 66

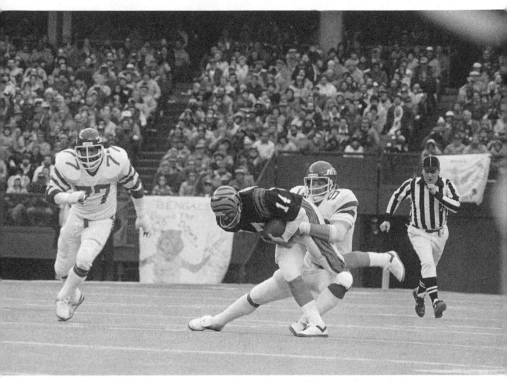

Bengals quarterback Ken Anderson (No. 14) is pulled down by Marty Lyons (No. 93) for a loss in the third quarter of action on Sunday, January 9, 1983, in Cincinnati, Ohio. Since retiring from football, Lyons has gone on to do a great deal of charity work.

quarterback sacks in 1981. Lyons had six sacks that season, despite missing time due to a hamstring injury.

He again missed time in 1982 due to a bad hamstring. But when he played, he was a difference-maker. The Jets made the play-offs that season, and Lyons made a sack in each of the team's three playoff games. And he led the team with 12 tackles in the AFC Championship Game loss to the Miami Dolphins.

Injuries would punctuate Lyons' career. He missed four games due to shoulder surgery in 1986, but he came back strong to start 13 games in 1987. He then led the team in sacks in 1988 when he had a career-high seven for the season.

Difficult Jets Trivia

Here's the big test of whether you paid attention while reading this book. These are questions that are tough, and reading this book would greatly aid your pursuit of having the correct answers.

1. Who scored the first touchdown in the organization's history?
2. What team did the Titans play in their first Thanksgiving Day appearance?
3. What was Charley Winner's relationship to Weeb Ewbank?
4. True or false: Don Maynard caught over 100 touchdowns during his 15-year career?
5. How many seasons did Lou Holtz coach the Jets?
6. How many games did the Jets win during Rich Kotite's tenure as Jets head coach?
7. What was the name of the original owner of the New York Titans, the team that became the Jets?
8. What are the four numbers retired by the Jets, and who wore them?
9. Who played linebacker for the Jets in 1964, was a part Choctaw-Chickasaw Native American, and later became a professional wrestler?
10. For his performance in what movie did Joe Namath get nominated for a Golden Globe in 1971?

Answers:

1. Al Dorow
2. Dallas Texans
3. Son-in-law
4. False
5. One
6. Four
7. Harry Wismer

8. Nos. 12, 13, 73, and 80, which belonged to Joe Namath, Don Maynard, Joe Klecko, and Wayne Chrebet.
9. Wahoo McDaniel
10. *Norwood*

All told, Lyons underwent eight operations during his career.

A native of Takoma Park, Maryland, Lyons became a leader on the Jets and a demonstrative one at that. He knew how to get his teammates' attention, which he managed to do while trying to fire them up prior to a 1982 playoff game against the Raiders in the Los

Angeles Coliseum. Initially Lyons had planned to use a movie projector as his prop. But Jets coaches informed him that he would be fined if he decided to toss the projector through a window. So rather than incur the fine—but still managing to get his point across—Lyons punched a window. The Jets defeated the Raiders 17–14 that day to advance to the AFC Championship Game.

Lyons tore a bicep in a 1990 exhibition game against the Giants, which caused him to miss all of the 1990 season. Ultimately that injury would lead to the end of his career. He announced his retirement in February 1991.

When he retired, he had recorded 29 quarterback sacks in 147 games and had outlasted all of his fellow members of the New York Sack Exchange.

After retiring, Lyons became the Jets' radio analyst and chairman of the Marty Lyons Foundation, contributing as much off the field as he had on the field while playing for the Jets.

Sources

Books:

Eskenazi, Gerald. *Gang Green: An Irreverent Look Behind the Scenes at Thirty-Eight (Well, Thirty-Seven) Seasons of New York Jets Football Futility.* New York: Simon & Schuster, 1998.

Felser, Larry. *The Birth of the New NFL: How the 1966 NFL/AFL Merger Transformed Pro Football.* Guilford, CT: Lyons Press, 2008.

Gruver, Ed. *From Baltimore to Broadway: Joe, the Jets, and the Super Bowl III Guarantee.* Chicago: Triumph Books, 2009.

Gruver, Ed. *The American Football League: A Year-By-Year History, 1960–1969.* Jefferson, NC: McFarland & Company, Inc., 1997.

Johnson, Keyshawn and Shelly Smith. *Just Give Me the Damn Ball!: The Fast Times and Hard Knocks of an NFL Rookie.* New York: Grand Central Publishing, 1997.

Kriegel, Mark. *Namath: A Biography.* New York: Penguin Group, 2004.

Miller, Jeff. *Going Long: The Wild 10-Year Saga of the Renegade American Football League in the Words of Those Who Lived It.* New York: McGraw-Hill, 2003.

Rappoport, Ken. *The Little League That Could: A History of the American Football League.* Lanham, MD: Taylor Trade Publishing, 2010.

Sample, Johnny, Fred J. Hamilton, Sonny Schwartz, and Joe Namath. *Confessions of a Dirty Ballplayer.* New York: Dial Press, 1970.

Schapp, Richard and Joe Willie Namath. *I Can't Wait Until Tomorrow...'Cause I Get Better-Looking Every Day.* New York: Random House, 1969.

Shamsky, Art, Barry Zeman, Bob Costas, and Tom Seaver. *The Magnificent Seasons: How the Jets, Mets, and Knicks Made Sports History and Uplifted a City and the Country.* New York: Thomas Dunn Books, 2004.

Steidel, David. *Remember the AFL: The Ultimate Fan's Guide to the American Football League.* Cincinnati: Clerisy Press, 2008.

Newspapers and Magazines:
New York Times
Pittsburgh Post-Gazette
Sports Illustrated

Websites:
Bloomberg.com
Boston.com
Newyorkjets.com
Projo.com
Sports.espn.go.com
Sportsillustrated.cnn.com